A simple plan for effective Bible study

COME and DINE

D0807325

Richard Booker
author of *The Miracle of the Scarlet Thread*

Cover Photo: Vernon Sigl

A simple plan for effective Bible study

COME *and* DINE

Destiny Image Publishers
P.O. Box 351
Shippensburg, PA 17257

"Speaking to the Purposes of God for this Generation"

Scriptural quotations have been carefully selected from the following versions of the Bible:

King James Version (KJV)

The New King James Bible (New Testament), copyright © 1979, Thomas Nelson, Inc., Nashville, TN. (NKJ)

New International Version, copyright © 1978, New York International Bible Society. Used by permission. (NIV)

Revised Standard Version (RSV)

The Living Bible, copyright © 1971, Tyndale House Publishers, Wheaton, Il. Used by permission. (TLB)

COME*and*DINE

Library of Congress Catalog Number: 82-73508
International Standard Book Number: 1-56043-019-2
Destiny Image Publishers, Shippensburg, PA 17257

Acknowledgments

My love and gratitude to the following:

My wife, Peggy, for typing the manuscript and for being my most treasured and faithful Bible student.

The reviewers, who read the manuscript and gave helpful comments and needed encouragement.

All lovers of God's Word, who have helped me learn how to study the Scriptures for myself.

Contents

About the Author

Richard Booker is a Bible teacher who lives in Houston, Texas. His organization, Sounds of the Trumpet, Inc., provides Christian teachings through books, tapes, seminars, etc. Prior to his call to the teaching ministry, he was a computer consultant, climbing the corporate career ladder. His BS and MBA degrees from Louisiana Tech University prepared him well. His career became his god, and he spent ten years chasing that illusive idol, dragging his wife, Peggy, across the country with him.

During that time he lectured throughout the United States, Canada and Mexico, training over 1000 management and computer personnel. His more than twenty articles appeared in the leading computer publications. He was listed in *Who's Who in Computers and Automation, Who's Who in Training and Development,* and *The Dictionary of International Biography,* and he was a frequent speaker for the American Management Association.

He wanted to be king of the hill until he discovered that someone already occupied that spot. That someone was Jesus Christ. With this new insight, Richard began to study the Bible. He had read it before, but it had never been understandable to him. He couldn't find any common theme that connected it all together.

But with a new awareness of Jesus Christ, God began to show Richard how to feed himself with the Scriptures. His life was changed as he began to digest God's Word. He wrote *Come and Dine* to help you learn how to apply these same divine feeding habits to your own study of God's Word. He invites you now to—*Come and Dine.*

Preface

Have you ever wondered why you are on planet earth? We all have asked ourselves, "What is life all about? Where did I come from? Why am I here? Where am I going? Is there any meaning to it all?" The answer to these questions is: *Yes!* There *is* meaning and purpose in life. That meaning and purpose is to know God and live in His glory forever.

But how can we know God? If He's really there, He must be so far removed from us, that any understanding we would have of Him would only be the product of our own imaginations. And we would never know if these were right. Therefore, if we are to know God, He must take the initiative to reveal himself to us.

The good news is that God has taken the initiative. He has revealed himself to us in four ways. The first way is through *creation*. All of creation declares to us the existence of God.

Secondly, He has built within each of us a *God consciousness*. Whether we will admit it or not, we all have a sense, or a knowledge, that there is a God who created us to know Him.

But these general revelations of God only tell us something about Him. They do not really help us to know Him. So, God decided to reveal himself to us in a third way. He wrote His autobiography. It's called—*the Bible*. Through the pages of the Bible, we can come to know God and find the answers to the mysteries and deep questions about life.

Yet, even then, people have sometimes missed the spirit of God's autobiography. Therefore, God chose a fourth and final way to reveal himself to us. This is through the person of the *Lord Jesus Christ* who was God in the flesh. God gave us the Bible that we might know Him and become wise for salvation through faith in Jesus Christ.

God not only desires that we know Him, but that we also learn to walk with Him. We learn this, also, from the Bible. In its pages, God shows us the path we should walk, reveals when we are off the path, and helps us to get back on the path. He also teaches us how to stay on the path.

So, yes, we can know God and live in His glory forever. We can learn to walk with Him—but only as we give ourselves to the written revelation of who He is. The Bible is that revelation of the one true God and how we may know Him and walk with Him through Jesus Christ.

God says, in the Bible, that if we will seek Him with our whole heart, we will find Him. He is waiting for you. *Will you open the Bible and your heart and get to know Him?*

A simple plan for effective Bible study

COME *and* DINE

Richard Booker
author of *The Miracle of the Scarlet Thread*

Cover Photo: Vernon Sigl

1
Introduction

The Bible makes a most amazing claim for itself. It claims to be the written Word of God. This is so bold that it requires our personal investigation. If the Bible is not what it claims to be, then we should not give serious consideration to its teachings. *However, if the Bible reasonably supports its claims, we should devote the rest of our lives to reading, studying and applying its teachings to our lives.* We should get to know the God of the Bible.

Since the Bible claims to be from God, it often speaks of itself as having life-changing effects on those who will take in its words. It's compared to a hammer that is able to break up our hard hearts. A mirror that can show us our sins. Water that can wash our sins away. Milk to make us strong.

Christians believe that the Bible does support its claims. They believe it is the written Word of God. *However, few Christians know how to read and study the Bible for*

1

themselves. Many do not personally experience these life-changing effects which the Bible claims for itself. Bible study becomes a drudgery that leaves them dry, confused and even more frustrated. Many give up and settle for a sermon on Sunday morning from the preacher. Others persevere but seldom receive the life-changing effects which God has for them.

Why I Wrote This Book

This describes my past Christian experience. For many years I tried to find life in the words of the Bible, yet they never came alive in my spirit. But in God's own time, He began to put a desire in my heart to study His Word. As I responded to this desire, God showed me how to feed myself with the Scriptures in ways that helped me to receive life from His Word. *I wrote this book to help you learn these same divine feeding habits, so that you might be better able to read, study and understand the Bible for yourself.* Personal Bible study is absolutely necessary for a Christian to grow in the faith. It is good to read books about the Bible, but we must go beyond that and read the Bible for ourselves. It's great to hear sermons from the Bible, but we must hear the voice of God for ourselves, through our own personal Bible study.

And to the Christian, Jesus has given the Holy Spirit who will teach us and lead us as we seek to know the truths of God. (See John 14:26; 16:13.) It is my prayer that the Holy Spirit will use the principles presented in this book to help you do just that.

A Look at What's Ahead

You will begin in chapter two by discovering *how the Bible is different* from every other book which has ever been written. People have a curiosity about the Bible. They may not read it, but they are interested in why it is so special and different. We'll start by examining the claims of the Bible and how the Bible backs up its claims with overwhelming evidence.

2

In chapter three, you'll find out *how God brought the Bible together.* The Bible was written by many authors over a long period of time. It consists of sixty-six different books. How do we know that these books are from God? We'll see in this chapter.

In chapter four, you'll follow the story of the Old Testament and see how the books in this part of the Bible are organized. In doing so, you will briefly *survey every book in the Old Testament* and come to understand the purpose of each one, and how they all fit together. You will also see how they point to Jesus Christ and discover what meaning they have for you today.

In chapter five you will learn how the New Testament books are organized. You will briefly *survey every New Testament book* and become aware of each one's primary theme and basic message concerning the Lord Jesus Christ.

In chapter six, you will take an adventurous journey back in time to see *how we got our English Bible.* For many years, the Bible was a closed book, because it was not in the language people could read. Then God began to raise up men to translate the Bible into the English language. Many people gave their lives so that we could read the Bible for ourselves, and this knowledge should encourage you to read it more diligently.

With this important background, you'll then be ready to move on to chapter seven, which will help you learn *how to get into the Bible.* You'll be encouraged as you see the blessings God has promised to impart to you through Bible study. You will also learn what attitude is necessary in Bible study in order to hear from God.

As we continue with chapter eight, you'll become aware of the fine difference between reading and studying. Then you'll look at six essentials that will help you *read the Bible more effectively.*

In chapter nine, you'll learn how to *meditate on the Scriptures.* It's very important to read the Bible on a regular basis. But just reading is not enough. We must also learn to meditate on God's Word. In this chapter, you'll become acquainted with the meditation process and discover the steps to meaningful meditation.

In chapter ten, you will find out how to *study a book* in the Bible. One of the keys to studying the Bible is that your study must be systematic and consistent. In this chapter, you'll examine a plan that will help you apply these keys to the study of a Bible book.

Then you'll continue in chapter eleven by examining a plan to help you *study a topic* in the Bible. You'll learn the basic steps involved and how to apply them. You'll also find some helpful outlines to aid you in your study of the basic teachings of the Christian faith.

In chapter twelve, you'll discover the five principles that will help you to *better understand* the Bible. Many people do not have confidence that they can understand the Bible. But your confidence will soar as you learn these principles for correctly interpreting God's Word.

Finally in chapter thirteen, you'll become acquainted with six basic *Bible study aids* that will help you to enlarge your knowledge of the Scriptures and make your Bible study richer and more meaningful.

In addition, there are *review exercises* at the end of each of the following chapters to help you highlight and reinforce what you have learned. The review exercises may be completed on an individual or group basis.

What Is God's Word to You?

As you continue to read the pages of this book, I pray that God will establish and increase your love and zeal for His Word and open the eyes of your understanding to know Him in a way that will enable you to walk in newness of life.

King David found the Word of God to be more desired than fine gold and sweeter than pure honey from the honeycomb. May you find it to be that way as well.

4

2

What Makes the Bible Different?

About the year 1526 BC, Pharaoh's daughter found a Hebrew baby boy hidden among the reeds in a homemade waterproof basket, along the banks of the Nile River. She named him Moses. Moses grew up in Pharaoh's household. As a young boy growing to manhood, he had the best that Egypt could offer. He had all the privileges of position, power and wealth. He had a brilliant mind and was given the best education Egypt had available. He was at the top of his class. He learned all of the wisdom of Egypt and was mighty in words and deeds. He was a great prince of Egypt.

But when Moses learned his true identity, he killed an Egyptian who was mistreating a Hebrew slave. For this, Moses had to flee Egypt and lived in exile for forty years. One day while he was walking in the desert near Mount Sinai, the Creator God appeared to Moses in a burning bush. God called Moses to go back to Egypt to lead the

Hebrews out of slavery to a land He had promised them. God also intructed Moses to record the things he had learned from God and from those Hebrews who knew the truths of God. Moses then spoke God's words to the Egyptians. He began to write, *"In the beginning God . . . ."*

From that day until now, the world has scoffed at Moses' words. World leaders down through the ages have tried to destroy the Bible. They have failed, yet the attack continues. People of the world deny the Bible's divine authority. They try to destroy it intellectually. They ridicule, mock and laugh at believers. The usual justification for this disbelief is that the modern world is too sophisticated, enlightened, rational and intelligent to accept the Bible.

Yet, the Bible is different. Regardless of what a person may believe about it, we all have to agree that the Bible is unique. No other book has survived history and attacks against it as the Bible. No other book has influenced civilization and individual lives like the Bible. No other book has been translated into as many languages and has been read by as many people as the Bible. And what other book but the Bible would millions of people all over the world give their lives to preserve and distribute?

A Book You Can Believe

In this chapter we're going to discover what makes the Bible different. And we'll see that, contrary to popular opinion, *believing in the Bible for what it claims to be, is the most intelligent, rational decision a person can make.* I'm talking about facts. Overwhelming facts. Facts about the Bible that demand any intelligent person to acknowledge its divine authority. Once you examine the facts, you will see that people who pretend to reject the Bible, from an intellectual argument, are being dishonest. They are really rejecting it from their hearts which has caused their minds to become blinded to truth. And while professing themselves to be wise, they have become utter fools.

Yet, for those who do believe, God does not expect blind faith. But He has left us with His divine fingerprints on the pages of history and these bear witness to the Scriptures as being the inspired Word of God. *We are now going to consider five characteristics of the Bible which make it different from all other books.*

1. Title, Subject and Author

The first characteristic is the *title, subject and author* of the Bible. To emphasize this uniqueness, let's take a stroll down to the public library. Libraries are supposed to be quiet. So, as you open the door and go in, you are careful not to make a disturbance.

Once inside, you find tens of thousands of books. There are books on every subject imaginable. You see books on art, music, philosophy, law and other topics. And there are the how-to books which cover every conceivable topic from how to grow roses to how to build computers.

And these books are sectioned off to help you find them. Possibly you stop in one section, take a book off the shelf, turn to page one and read the first line to see what it's about.

You might read something like the following: "In recent years there have been many reports of a growing impatience with psychiatry . . . ." This book is going to tell you something about your mind. You may or may not be interested in it. If you are, you will check out the book and read it. If not, you'll put the book back on the shelf and keep on walking through the aisle.

You proceed to pick up another book and read the following first line: "If I ask you what the most important thing in life is to you, many of you would say it's your future earning power." Well, this book is going to tell you how to make money. If you are like most people, you'll probably check it out.

As you continue to browse, you pick up book after book on subject after subject. Some of them you put back on the shelf, and others you may borrow to take home.

The Book of Books

One of the books you pick up seems like all the others. It's merely paper and print bound together like every other book. But then you notice the title. It's called, *Holy Bible*. This book claims to be holy. That means it is separate from any other book that has ever been written. There's no other book like this one.

As you think about it, you can't remember ever reading a book that claimed to be holy. Why even the science and philosophy books from college don't have "holy" written on them. But this book does. And it doesn't try to hide it or catch you off guard. It just comes right out and boldly proclaims it on the front cover: Holy Bible. Therefore, none can say that they don't know what the Bible claims.

So, you rather hurriedly take the book off the shelf, open to the first page and read, "In the beginning God . . . ." *This book is going to tell you about God!* The subject is "How to Find God." This automatically makes it the most unique how-to book in the world. The other books you looked at tell you about something that God has created. But this book is about the Creator himself. This book claims to have the answer to the meaning and purpose of life. *Therefore, it is either the most important book in the world, or the most useless.*

For centuries and centuries scientific investigation and human reason have been trying to find out how to get to God. Yet, they have failed. Now you're holding in your own hand the book that claims to have the answer.

The Word of God

So, quickly you thumb through the pages to find out who is the author. Finally, you come to 2 Timothy 3:16 which reads, "All Scripture is given by inspiration of God . . ." (NKJ).

Now this says that God is the author of the Bible. Well, that makes sense because only God would know the unsearchable truths of God. The creature would not know all there is about the Creator and His creation. Only the Creator would.

So, this book claims that every word in it is inspired by God.

This means that it doesn't just claim to contain the Word of God, if you can find it among the pages. But the claim is that the whole book is the written Word of God. Of course, you cannot pick out parts you like and ignore the parts you don't like. But all of the Bible claims to be the written Word of God. *Regardless of what a person might believe about the Bible, this is what it claims.*

One of the greatest philosophers of all times was a man by the name of Plato. Plato lived about 400 years before Jesus was born. One day Plato said to his students, "We must lay hold of the best of human opinion in order to sail over the dangerous sea of life; unless we find a stronger boat or some sure word of God which will more surely and safely carry us."

Your Personal Investigation

The Bible claims to be that "some sure word of God." Of all the books in the world, this is the one book you cannot afford to put back on the shelf. *You must check it out for yourself to see if it stands up to its claims.*

Oh, you've heard what people have said about the Bible. Perhaps you've even repeated some of the things you have heard, such as: "Why, the Bible was just written by a bunch of men. It's just an old book, full of nice stories for old ladies and little kids. But really it has no relevance today. And you can't take it literally. Besides, it's your own interpretation that counts. So, you can take the parts you like and leave the parts you don't like."

This is the one book you must read for yourself. The critics' reviews are not good enough. Not this time. Because this book claims to be about you and God. *So, if you are searching for the truth to the meaning and purpose of life, in order to make a rational, intelligent decision, you must examine this book for yourself.* You must come to your own first-hand conclusion.

2. Continuity

The second characteristic about the Bible that makes it

different is its *continuity*. By continuity, I mean that the Bible tells one, continuous story from beginning to ending.

Here is the story. The Bible says that God is perfect in all of His being while man is not perfect. Man has within him a rebellious, self-centered nature which God calls sin. This sin nature separates man from God, not only in this life, but in the life after this one. Thus, the consequence of sin is death—body, soul and spirit.

God must see that the consequence is carried out because He is a God of perfect justice. And there's nothing man can do to remove the consequence.

But God is also a God of perfect love. He loves us in spite of our sins. And because He loves us, God has taken the initiative to come to the earth and suffer the consequences for us. He did this by supernaturally preparing for himself a body in the womb of a virgin. His name was Jesus of Nazareth. They referred to Him as Emmanuel, which means—God with us.

Jesus lived a perfect life, never committing any sin. But He died as the innocent, substitutionary sacrifice for the sins of the world. Yet, because He never sinned, death couldn't hold Him in the grave. So, after three days and three nights, Jesus was resurrected. He appeared to more than 500 people for forty days and then ascended back to heaven where He now sits on the throne of God as King of kings and Lord of lords. If we will receive Him into our lives, we will partake of His divine nature and live with Him forever in glory.

This is the story of the Bible. It's the subject from Genesis to Revelation and everything in between. It's the *master theme of the Bible*. It's the single scarlet thread holding it all together.

Unity of the Bible

And, although not apparent on the surface, the Bible tells this story with *perfect unity and harmony*. What makes that unique is that this story was told over a 1600-year period (1500 BC to 100 AD). To further complicate matters, over forty writers recorded the story. Can you imagine over forty different authors writing over a 1600-year period, yet telling their story with perfect unity and harmony?

And these writers weren't from the same neighborhood either. Therefore, they would not be conditioned by their environments to think alike. But they would see things differently because they were from every walk of life. For example, Moses, as we have discussed, was a well-educated political leader who had studied in the universities of Egypt. In contrast, Peter was a fisherman with little formal education. Joshua was a military leader. Luke was a doctor. Solomon was a king, while Matthew was a tax collector. David tells his part of the story in times of war. Jeremiah tells his in a dungeon. John writes from an island, while Paul writes from a Roman jail.

The story was written in three languages (Hebrew, Aramaic, and Greek), on three continents (Asia, Africa, and Europe).

Beyond a Shadow of a Doubt

There were many writers separated by language, culture, geography, and other factors, writing on many controversial subjects. Nonetheless, somehow they all tell the same story. *Is this humanly possible?* We can't even get the finest of minds, all experts on the same subject, living at the same time, in the same place, with similiar backgrounds, to agree on even one controversial subject, but the Bible speaks about many controversial subjects with perfect unity and harmony. The Bible is different because of its continuity, its internal consistency.

3. Reliably Preserved

The third unique characteristic about the Bible is that it has been *reliably preserved.* God has preserved His Word. We do not have any original manuscripts of the Bible. God probably didn't preserve any original manuscripts because, if we had them, we would probably worship them. But He has faithfully preserved His Word for us.

There are no original Old Testament manuscripts because

the newer copies were considered superior to the old. This was due to the fact that Hebrew scribes were so precise in preparing the newer copies. Therefore, the older copies were discarded. For a manuscript to be old was actually considered to be a disadvantage. We have no original New Testament manuscripts because the New Testament was written on a perishable material called "papyrus." We get our English word "paper" from the Greek word for papyrus.

The Overwhelming Evidence

What God has preserved from the ancient manuscripts is much more reliable and plentiful than any other ancient writing. For example, there are only five to ten copies of the writings of men such as Aristotle, Plato and Socrates. And there is a 1000 to 1500-year time gap between their original writings and the earliest copies we have of their writings. No one questions the authenticity of these writings.

The evidence to support the reliability of the Bible is overwhelming. There are approximately 5000 Greek manuscripts of the New Testament. Many of these manuscripts are within 200 to 300 years of the original writings. In addition, there are numerous early translations, as well as the writings of the early Christian leaders. We will discuss these topics more fully in chapter six.

But how about the Old Testament? The Old Testament was completed in about 400 BC. That's a long time ago. Just how reliable, then, is it? The answer to this question came in 1947 with the discovery of the Dead Sea Scrolls. The Dead Sea Scrolls are Hebrew manuscripts dating as far back as 200 BC. These writings consist of more than 40,000 fragments of almost every book in the Old Testament. When comparing the Dead Sea Scrolls with our modern manuscripts, scholars found absolutely no significant differences. For more details on this subject, you may want to read *Evidence That Demands a Verdict* by Josh McDowell (Campus Crusade for Christ, 1972).

The printing press was not invented until the 1450s. Until that time manuscripts were copied by hand. Of course, it's impossible for people to make copies for all those years without making mistakes. And they did make mistakes. But these mistakes were insignificant errors in spelling, grammar, etc.

Although many people may question the Bible's inspiration, no one who has studied its development can seriously challenge its reliability. *If a person disclaims the Bible from an intellectual viewpoint, he must also disclaim every ancient document which has ever been written, because the Bible is the most authenticated and reliable of all ancient books.*

4. Prophecies

The fourth unique characteristic about the Bible is its *prophecies.* There are many prophecies in the Bible about many different things. But the most important prophecies center around the person of the Lord Jesus Christ. There are approximately 300 definable prophecies about the coming Messiah. Jesus fulfilled thirty-three of these on the day He died.

We are now going to consider eight of these prophecies:

1. *Messiah to Be Born in Bethlehem.*

In the Old Testament we read, "O Bethlehem Ephrathah, you are but a small Judean village, yet you will be the birthplace of my King who is alive from everlasting ages past" (Mic. 5:2, TLB).

The New Testament says, "Jesus was born in the town of Bethlehem, in Judea, during the reign of King Herod . . ." (Matt. 2:1, TLB).

2. *Messiah to Be Preceded by a Messenger.*

The Old Testament states, "The voice of him that crieth in the wilderness, Prepare ye the way of the Lord, make straight in the desert a highway for our God" (Isa. 40:3, KJV).

The New Testament reads, "In those days John the Baptist came preaching in the wilderness of Judea and saying: 'Repent, for the Kingdom of Heaven is at hand!' For this is he who was spoken of by the prophet Isaiah saying: 'The voice of one crying in the wilderness: Prepare the way of the Lord, make His paths straight' " (Matt. 3:1-3, NKJ).

3. *Messiah to Enter Jerusalem on a Donkey.*

The Old Testament says, "Rejoice greatly, O daughter of Zion; shout, O daughter of Jerusalem: behold, thy King cometh unto thee: he is just, and having salvation; lowly, and riding upon an ass, and upon a colt the foal of an ass" (Zech. 9:9, KJV).

The New Testament states, "Tell the daughter of Zion, 'Behold, your King is coming to you, Humble, and sitting on a donkey, and a colt, the foal of a donkey' " (Matt. 21:5, NKJ).

4. *Messiah Betrayed by a Close Friend.*

The Old Testament reads, "Even my bosom friend in whom I trusted, who ate my bread, has lifted his heel against me" (Ps. 41:9, RSV).

The New Testament reads, "Judas Iscariot, who also betrayed him" (Matt. 10:4, KJV).

5. *Messiah Sold for Thirty Pieces of Silver.*

In the Old Testament it says, "So they weighed for my price thirty pieces of silver" (Zech. 11:12, KJV).

The New Testament fulfillment is, "Then Judas, who had betrayed Him, . . . brought back the thirty pieces of silver to the Chief priests and elders" (Matt. 27:3, NKJ).

6. *Messiah Silent Before His Accusers.*

The Old Testament states, "He was oppressed, and he was afflicted, yet he opened not his mouth" (Isa. 53:7, KJV).

The New Testament reads, "But Jesus said nothing, much to the governor's surprise" (Matt. 27:14, TLB).

7. *Messiah's Hands and Feet Pierced.*

The Old Testament says, "They pierced my hands and my feet" (Ps. 22:16, KJV).

The New Testament fulfillment is, "There they crucified him" (Luke 23:33, KJV). (When Jesus was crucified, His hands and feet were pierced.)

8. *Messiah Numbered With Transgressors.*

The Old Testament reads, "And he was numbered with the transgressors" (Isa. 53:12, KJV).

The New Testament fulfillment reads, "Then were there two thieves crucified with him" (Matt. 27:38, KJV).

God's Plan or Chance?

Peter Stoner, in his book, *Science Speaks* (Moody Press, 1963), calculated the probability that any one person would just happen to fulfill these eight prophecies by chance or coincidence. He found that the probability was one in ten to the seventeenth power. That's a one with seventeen zeros after it. This is a number so big that we can't even begin to understand it. Mr. Stoner gives the following illustration to explain it.

Assume that you live in the state of Texas, and you fill up a Texas-size dump truck with silver dollars in the amount of ten to the seventeeth power. Then you dump these silver dollars across the entire state of Texas, two feet deep. Somewhere out there in the middle of those silver dollars is one silver dollar with a little red dot on it. You put a blindfold over someone's eyes and send them out to find that one silver dollar with the little red dot on it. The individual gets only one chance. That the person would pick up the one silver dollar with the red dot staggers the mind, because such a likelihood is highly improbable.

Likewise, anyone would be foolish to believe that just these eight prophecies alone could be given by human wisdom and fulfilled by one man through coincidence. There is only one reasonable explanation. The apostle Peter gives us the answer with these words, "For no prophecy recorded in Scripture was ever thought up by the prophet himself. It was the Holy Spirit within these godly men who gave them true messages from God" (2 Pet. 1:21, TLB).

The prophet Isaiah said, "The grass withers, the flower fades; but the word of our God will stand forever" (Isa. 40:8, RSV). If Plato were alive today, we could tell him we have found that "some sure word of God." And as we apply it to our lives, *it surely will carry us through the dangerous sea of life.*

5. The Bible Changes Lives

And that brings us to the fifth characteristic of the Bible which makes it different. The Bible *changes people's lives.* God is a life-changing God. Therefore, any book He wrote would be full of His life breathed into the very words themselves. And when people seek to know God, the Word of God comes alive in their hearts. And as the Word of God forms and grows in them, the Holy Spirit transforms them by renewing their minds and changing the desires of their hearts.

King David said it this way, "Wherewithal shall a young man cleanse his way? by taking heed thereto according to thy word. With my whole heart have I sought thee: O let me not wander from thy commandments. Thy word have I hid in my heart, that I might not sin against thee" (Ps. 119:9-11, KJV).

The Word of God has changed my life. If you will open your heart to God, it will change yours as well.

Chapter 2—What Makes the Bible Different?

Review Exercise 1

1. List five characteristics of the Bible that makes it different from any other book.

   a.
   b.
   c.
   d.
   e.

2. Explain the significance of each of the five characteristics.

   a.

   b.

   c.

   d.

   e.

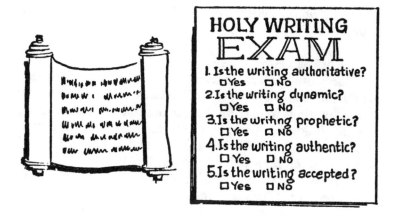

3

How the Bible Came Together

In our previous chapter, we learned that the Bible was written over a 1600-year period. There were many other things written during that time period also. Man needed to know which writings were from God and which were not. You wouldn't want to get yourself thrown to the lions for something somebody in the back room wrote. Neither would you want to run the risk of missing something from God.

Thus, it was necessary for God to separate what He had directed to be written from what man had written out of his own mind. But by the time God had said everything He wanted to say, His Word was scattered throughout many different books. So, God moved upon men to bring His word together under one cover, as one book.

And God supervised the entire assembling process, although He used men to actually do the work. God himself put the Bible together. Man's part was only to recognize these writings which God had already ordained. *This would be those books which contained the very stamp of divine authority.*

The Ancient Test

Man would test the ancient writings to see which were from God and which were not. To guide him in recognizing which writings were from God, man subjected each writing to the following five-point test mentioned by Norman Geisler & William Nix in their book, *A General Introduction to the Bible* (Moody Press, 1968).

1. Is the writing authoritative? Does it declare the message, "Thus says the Lord"?
2. Is the writing dynamic? Does it change lives?
3. Is the writing prophetic? Was it written by a man of God?
4. Is the writing authentic? Can it be proven beyond doubt?
5. Is the writing recognized by the people during its time as being from God?

We see that a bunch of old men didn't just sit around and flip a coin to determine what was from God and what wasn't. But God directed the entire project with man only recognizing what God had already ordained.

God's Word Comes Together

As it turned out, man recognized sixty-six different books as being from God. These books were put under one cover and became what we know as the Holy Bible.

The Bible was divided into two parts. The first division was called the Old Testament. It contains thirty-nine books. The second division was called the New Testament. It contains twenty-seven books.

The Old Testament

The books in the Old Testament were written from about 1500-400 BC. The last book in the Old Testament was the book of Malachi. It is still the last book in the Old Testament—in the English Bible. The Hebrews, on the other hand, placed the book of Chronicles at the end of the Old Testament and included Malachi earlier in the sequence of books. Therefore, the Hebrew Old Testament started with Genesis and ended with Chronicles.

Here's why this is important. *Jesus and the apostles considered the thirty-nine books which make up the Old Testament to be the Word of God.* They often quoted from a body of writings called the Scriptures. The Old Testament formed the Scriptures from which they were quoting. In fact, the New Testament contains about 300 quotes from the Old Testament.

Jesus confirmed what He considered to be the complete Old Testament in a statement recorded in the book of Luke. He said that the blood of the prophets would be on the religious leaders' hands, "From the blood of Abel to the blood of Zechariah . . ." (Luke 11:51, NKJ).

In the Old Testament, Abel was the first martyr as recorded in Genesis 4:8. The last martyr mentioned in the Old Testament, according to the Hebrew sequence of books, was Zechariah, and his martyrdom is recorded in 2 Chronicles 24:21. Jesus was saying (in Luke 11:51) that He considered the complete Old Testament to be Genesis to Chronicles and all the books in between.

The Silent Years

There were about 400 years between the time when the Old Testament was completed and the time when the New Testament began. During this time God did not speak any new word to the Hebrew people. There were many voices, but none were from God. Fourteen books were written during this "silent" period. These books became known as the Apocrypha. The word "apocrypha" means "writings of doubtful authenticity or authorship." It refers to writings that do not carry the stamp of divine authority.

The Roman Catholic Church included eleven of these books as part of their Old Testament. However, the

Protestant denominations have rejected them because: the Hebrews didn't recognize them; Jesus didn't recognize them; the apostles didn't recognize them; the early Church leaders didn't recognize them; they didn't pass the five-point test; and the Catholics themselves didn't recognize them until 1546 AD, at the peak of the Protestant Reformation. *The books in the Protestant Old Testament are the same as the original Hebrew Old Testament, although not all of the books are in the same sequence.*

In 70 AD the Jewish Temple was destroyed and the people were scattered into various lands. Also, about that time, there appeared a number of writings from a group of people called Christians. Of course, no Jew wanted any of these Christian writings to somehow get into "their" Bible. So, it became necessary for the Jewish religious leaders to officially recognize those books which had been ordained by God. *Thus, in 90 AD, the Jews officially defined, recognized and confirmed the books in the Old Testament to be the inspired Word of God.*

The New Testament

The New Testament was written about 45-95 AD. It is important to realize that some of the New Testament writers were eyewitnesses to what they were writing about.

Peter wrote, "For we have not followed cunningly devised fables, when we made known unto you the power and coming of our Lord Jesus Christ, but were eyewitnesses of his majesty" (2 Pet. 1:16, KJV).

John wrote, ". . . I myself have seen him with my own eyes and listened to him speak. I have touched him with my own hands" (1 John 1:1, TLB).

Not only were they eyewitnesses, but so were the people to whom they were writing and speaking. Now think about that for a moment. There's a big difference in someone trying to convince someone else that they saw something, and in someone being reminded of what was seen by both parties.

Peter preached a sermon which brings out this point.

Luke records it for us in the book of Acts, "Men of Israel, hear these words: Jesus of Nazareth, a Man attested by God to you by miracles, wonders and signs which God did through Him in your midst, as you yourselves know" (Acts 2:22 NKJ).

Peter reminds the great crowd of people how Jesus performed miracles right in their midst. They all knew what he was saying about Jesus was true. Now, how did they respond? Luke says, ". . . and the same day about three thousand souls were added to them" (verse 41).

When Paul made an appeal for his life before King Agrippa, he reminded the king that he was familiar with the events in the life of Jesus (See Acts 26:26). Paul also wrote to the Corinthians about how more than 500 people saw Jesus after He was resurrected and that many of these people were still alive (See 1 Cor. 15:6).

Now many of these people hated Jesus. They hated the apostles and what they were writing as the New Testament. And if the statements about Jesus were not true, the people would have disputed them. They were looking for just any excuse to discredit Jesus and the writings of the apostles. But none could. They knew it was all true because they were all eyewitnesses.

But just as with the Old Testament, the New Testament had to be officially defined, recognized and confirmed. Several events sped up this process. One was the writings of the early Church fathers which had to be distinguished from the writings which were directly inspired by God. Also in 140 AD, a heretic named Marcion developed his own New Testament and tried to pass it off as the real thing. Then in 303 AD, the Roman Emperor, Diocletian, attempted to do away with all the Christians by burning them at the stake and destroying their writings. Nobody is going to volunteer for that unless they know without a doubt that they are burning for the Word of God. *So, finally in 393 AD, the New Testament was officially established.*

The Master Theme of the Bible
God has given His Word to us in the Book of books—the

Bible. And, as we've mentioned, the two divisions in the Bible are called the Old Testament and the New Testament. The word "testament" comes from a Latin word, *testamentum. The more precise word for these two divisions, however, is "covenant."* The Bible, therefore, is really the story of an Old Covenant and a New Covenant.

In the Bible, the word "covenant" means a binding agreement between two parties. The word actually means to "cut covenant." By definition, it is an agreement to "cut a covenant by the shedding of blood and walking between pieces of flesh." *The two divisions in the Bible are about an old blood covenant and a new blood covenant.*

A blood covenant between two parties is the closest, the most enduring, the most solemn and the most sacred of all compacts. It absolutely cannot be broken. When you enter into a blood covenant with someone, you promise to give them your life, your love and your protection forever. For a fuller discussion of the blood covenant, I encourage you to read another book I have written, *The Miracle of the Scarlet Thread* (Bridge Publishing, 1981).

And although the Bible consists of sixty-six different books, they all tell one central story. The story is that God has taken the initiative to enter into a blood covenant with man through the Lord Jesus Christ. *The covenant in the blood of Jesus is the "scarlet thread" that runs through both testaments.*

In the old blood covenant, God says that at a point in the future, He would enter into a new blood covenant with us. In fact, the entire Old Testament is simply a picture of God's salvation message in Jesus Christ. But the picture is in shadow form, represented by what seems to be meaningless rituals, customs, places, names and unrelated happenings. *But they are all individual pieces of the same picture.* Now a shadow isn't the real thing. But it points you to the real thing. God painted a shadow of himself in the Old Testament that pointed everyone to Him when He would come to cut the covenant in the New Testament. And every believer offered an innocent substitutionary sacrifice to cover their sins and point them into the future when God himself, through Jesus Christ, would come to take their sins away. He would be the once and for all perfect sacrifice.

You see, God had planned, that in His own appointed time, He would prepare for himself a body just like ours and become one with His creation. Since He is God, He naturally knew everything He would do when He became one with us. He knew where He would be born. He knew by what name He would be called. He knew everything about the details of His life. He even knew how He would die. Therefore, He painted this shadow of himself in the Old Testament so that everybody would recognize Him when He arrived on the scene. *This is how the entire Old Testament points to Jesus.*

A Word From Jesus

Now Jesus, himself, confirmed that this is what the entire Old Testament is about. By the time Jesus came along, the Jews had divided the Old Testament into three sections. These were the Law of Moses, the Prophets and the Psalms. When someone used these three references, they were referring to the complete Old Testament.

After Jesus was resurrected, He appeared to His disciples in Jerusalem and said, "This is what I told you while I was still with you: Everything must be fulfilled that is written about me in the Law of Moses, the Prophets, and the Psalms" (Luke 24:44, NIV).

With this statement, Jesus was claiming that the Old Testament was about himself. The disciples must have looked puzzled, so Jesus explained what the Old Testament writers said about Him. Luke records it for us: "Then he [Jesus] opened their minds so they could understand the Scriptures. He told them, 'This is what is written: The Christ [Messiah] will suffer and rise from the dead on the third day, and repentance and forgiveness of sins will be preached in his name to all nations, beginning at Jerusalem" (Luke 24:45-46, NIV).

Jesus opened their minds by telling them the key for

understanding the Scriptures. He told His disciples that the Old Testament writers wrote of His crucifixion and resurrection for the forgiveness of sins. *This is how the two testaments are linked together.* They both tell this one story. The Old Testament foretells its happening. The New Testament tells that it did happen. The people who looked forward to this happening were saved from their sins through faith in God's Word. And everyone who looks back to it as having been fulfilled in Jesus Christ is saved in the same way.

This is what Jesus wanted us to know when He said, "Don't misunderstand why I have come—it isn't to cancel the laws of Moses and the warnings of the prophets. No, I came to fulfill them, and to make them all come true" (Matt. 5:17, TLB).

The Bible is an orderly, progressive, unfolding revelation from God of the blood covenant He has entered into with man through the Lord Jesus Christ.

Jesus in Every Book of the Bible

Jesus also appeared, after His resurrection, to two men on the road to Emmaus, a city about seven miles from Jerusalem. These men were followers of Jesus and were saddened by His death. At first they didn't recognize Him.

But after walking with them for a short way, Jesus began to explain the Scriptures to them and how all the Scriptures point to Him. Jesus said to them, " 'You are such foolish, foolish people! You find it so hard to believe all that the prophets wrote in the Scriptures! Wasn't it clearly predicted by the prophets that the Messiah would have to suffer all these things before entering his time of glory?' Then Jesus quoted them passage after passage from the writings of the prophets, beginning with the book of Genesis and going right on through the Scriptures, explaining what the passages meant and what they said about himself" (Luke 24:25-27, TLB).

That must have been some teaching session. Jesus showed them the "scarlet thread" of the covenant in His blood

throughout the Old Testament. I believe Jesus must have
said something like the following:

In Genesis	I'm the Seed of Woman
In Exodus	I'm the Passover Lamb
In Leviticus	I'm the Perfect Sacrifice
In Numbers	I'm the Lifted-Up One
In Deuteronomy	I'm the True Prophet
In Joshua	I'm the Captain of Your Salvation
In Judges	I'm the Deliverer
In Ruth	I'm the Near Kinsman
In Samuel	I'm the King
In Kings	I'm the King
In Chronicles	I'm the King
In Ezra	I'm the Faithful Scribe
In Nehemiah	I'm the Restorer
In Esther	I'm the Advocate
In Job	I'm the Ever-Living Redeemer
In Psalms	I'm the New Song
In Proverbs	I'm the Wisdom of God
In Ecclesiastes	I'm the Goal of Life
In Song of Solomon	I'm the Lover of Your Soul
In Isaiah	I'm the Suffering Servant
In Jeremiah	I'm the Righteous Branch
In Lamentations	I'm the Weeping Prophet
In Ezekiel	I'm the Glory of God
In Daniel	I'm the Smiting Stone
In Hosea	I'm the Forgiving Bridegroom
In Joel	I'm the Giver of the Spirit
In Amos	I'm the Builder of the City
In Obadiah	I'm the Savior
In Jonah	I'm the First-Born From the Dead
In Micah	I'm the Ruler of All Ages
In Nahum	I'm the Avenger
In Habakkuk	I'm the God of Your Salvation
In Zephaniah	I'm in Your Midst
In Haggai	I'm the Restorer of the Kingdom
In Zechariah	I'm the Priest on the Throne
In Malachi	I'm the Sun of Righteousness
In Matthew	I'm the King of the Jews
In Mark	I'm the Servant
In Luke	I'm the Son of Man
In John	I'm the Son of God
In Acts	I'm the Giver of the Spirit
In Romans	I'm the Justifier

In Corinthians	I'm the Giver of Gifts
In Galatians	I'm the Liberator
In Ephesians	I'm the Exalted One
In Philippians	I'm the Strength and Joy
In Colossians	I'm the Head of All Things
In Thessalonians	I'm the Coming One
In Timothy and Titus	I'm the Faithful Pastor
In Philemon	I'm the Friend
In Hebrews	I'm the New Covenant
In James	I'm the Great Physician
In Peter	I'm the Cornerstone
In John	I'm Love and Light
In Jude	I'm the Preserver
In Revelation	I'm the King of Kings

Jesus Christ is the Alpha and Omega; the Beginning and the Ending; the First and the Last; the Root and Offspring of David; the Amen; the Beloved; the Door into Heaven; the Way, the Truth and the Life; the Ancient of Days; the Bright and Morning Star; the Resurrection and the Life.

He is the Bread of Life; the Horn of our Salvation; the Lord of Hosts; the Hope of Glory; the Lamb slain from the foundation of the world; the One who was and is and is to come; the Almighty.

He is Wonderful; Counselor; Prince of Peace; the Everlasting Father; the Mighty God.

Chapter 3—How the Bible Came Together

Review Exercise 2

1. List the five points man used as a guide to recognize which ancient writings were from God.

   a.
   b.
   c.
   d.
   e.

2. Explain how Jesus established what He considered to be the complete Old Testament.

3. State what New Testament witness gave the most credibility to the words of the New Testament writers.

4. Briefly explain the master theme of the Bible.

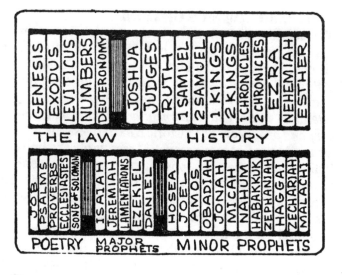

THE LAW   HISTORY

POETRY   MAJOR PROPHETS   MINOR PROPHETS

4

How the Old Testament Is Organized

Many times throughout the course of our lives, we have to learn about things that are new to us. But how do we begin? The best way is to get a general overview of the subject. The overview gives us a broad understanding of the subject; thus, we are able to see how the parts are related. Many Christians feel somewhat bewildered and intimidated by the Bible because they don't have this general orientation. And they get frustrated trying to put all the pieces together while they are drowning in the details. *So, in this chapter, we are going to see how the Old Testament is organized and take a general survey of each of the thirty-nine books with a brief statement about their purpose, time of writing, how they point to Jesus and their relevance to us.* Then we will continue on in the next chapter with the New Testament.

How the Old Testament Is Organized

We mentioned in our previous chapter that, by the time of Jesus, the Jews had divided the Old Testament into three divisions. These were the Law of Moses, the Prophets and the Psalms. These divisions were based on the types of literature employed within the books. *The three basic types of literature in the Old Testament are historical narratives, poetry and prophecy.* The historical narratives were referred to as the Law of Moses because Moses wrote the books in this division and the major portion of this section tells about God giving the Law to Moses and the Hebrew people. The books of poetry were identified as the Psalms because the book of Psalms was the first and longest book in this division. The third division was called the Prophets because they were written by men who held the office of prophet. Jesus referred to these three divisions and said they pointed to Him (See Luke 24:44). *Later, this threefold division of the Old Testament was expanded to the following: The Law— History—Poetry—Major Prophets—Minor Prophets.*

The Law

The Law includes the first five books of the Bible (Genesis through Deuteronomy). They téll a continuous story beginning with the creation of man and concluding with the Hebrews getting ready to go in and take the land which God had promised them. This covers the period of time in man's history from about 4000-1451 BC. *These five books are the foundation for the rest of the Bible. Therefore, we should be thoroughly familiar with their content.*

Genesis

Genesis is the book of beginnings. Here we find the account of creation. God's crowning piece in creation was man. God made man in His own image so that man could know God and walk with Him. But we learn that Adam and Eve sinned. Their sin separated them from God. *Yet God promised in Genesis 3:15 that He would come to the earth as a man to destroy the power of Satan and to save us from our sins.* The world soon became very wicked. God saw that man would not repent, so He destroyed the world with a great flood. Only Noah and his family were saved along with the animals God had told Noah to put in the ark. This was around the year 2400 BC. Noah had three sons: Shem, Ham and Japheth. God said He would come through the descendants of Shem (See Gen. 9:26).

Then, around the year 2000 BC, God entered into covenant with Abraham. God promised Abraham a land, to make his descendants a great nation and that He {God) would be of the seed of Abraham (See Gen. 12:1-9). But first, Abraham's descendants were to be exiled in Egypt for 400 years. Abraham and Sarah had a son named Isaac. *In Genesis 17:19, God further established His covenant with Isaac and then continued the covenant with his son Jacob, whose name was changed to Israel.* Israel had twelve sons which became known as the twelve tribes of Israel. God decreed that He would come into the world through the tribe of Judah (See Gen. 49:10). One of Jacob's sons was named Joseph. Joseph was sold by his brothers as a slave into Egypt. But he rose to a prominent position. Because of famine, Jacob and his family made their way to Egypt, where Joseph cared for them.

Exodus

While in Egypt, the Hebrews grew from a family of seventy to a nation of several million. Pharaoh felt threatened by them and made them slaves. God remembered His covenant with Abraham. He chose Moses to lead the Hebrew people out of Egyptian bondage around the year 1491 BC. God parted the Red Sea so they could escape. Along the way, God gave them the Ten Commandments, provided them with instructions for building a Tabernacle, established an elaborate system for making sacrifices and ordained a priesthood. Egypt was symbolic of the world system and Pharaoh represented Satan.

All of this pointed the Hebrew into the future when God would come in the person of the Lord Jesus Christ to set us free from bondage to Satan, sin and death. As the tabernacle of God in human form, He would live out the commandments as our example. He would give His own life as a perfect sacrifice and be a priest who would live forever to make intercession for us. He would write His laws on the tablets of our hearts. We would become the dwelling place of God in the Spirit. We would present our bodies to Him as a living sacrifice and minister as His priests to a lost world.

Leviticus

The theme of the book of Leviticus is that God is holy. Holy means separate. Before God led the Hebrews into their land, He wanted them to know that He was not like any of His creatures. He was different. Therefore, in order to walk with Him, the Hebrews had to be different from their heathen neighbors. God needed some visible means of showing this to His covenant people. So, He gave them laws regarding their conduct as a nation and as individuals. *These laws were designed to teach the people spiritual and moral truths about the nature and character of God.* Because He was different, they were to be different.

Jesus was different. No man lived like He lived. No man did what He did. No man talked like He talked. We must come to God through Him and we must also live a separated life from the world. We do this, not by trying to keep laws, but by yielding ourselves to the Lordship of Jesus Christ and walking in the power of the Holy Spirit.

Numbers

It was only a few-weeks journey from Egypt to the Promised Land. But it took the Hebrews forty years to make the trip. *This is because they failed to trust and obey God.* Instead, they murmured and complained. Then, when they got to the land, they sent in twelve spies to check it out. Ten of the spies reported that the inhabitants of the land were invincible. Only Joshua and Caleb were willing to go in and take the land as God had told them to do. But the people didn't listen. For this reason, they spent forty years wandering in the wilderness until that entire generation died, except for Joshua and Caleb.

Jesus said that He always did the will of the Father. He was obedient even unto death by crucifixion. He trusted the Father not to leave His soul in Hades nor to allow His body to decay in death. Therefore, God the Father has raised Him from the dead and set Him at His right hand with all authority and victory over sin, Satan and death. We too can have this victory with Christ if we will trust and obey God's Word.

Deuteronomy

The long wilderness journey had now come to an end, and it was time for the new generation of Hebrews who were born during the forty years to enter the Promised Land. This generation of Hebrews was not around when God made His covenant with their parents. *So, it was necessary for God to renew the covenant with them.* Moses called them together for one last time before he was to die, and he reminded them of how God had entered into covenant with their father Abraham. He recalled how God delivered them from Egypt and provided for them during their forty years of wandering. Then he reviewed the Ten Commandments and other laws God had given to them. He spoke of blessings if they would obey, but judgments if they would disobey. As a final act, Moses appointed Joshua as his successor.

Jesus is continually reminding us of our covenant with the Father. His words must be preached from generation to generation. We will be blessed as we remember His words and give ourselves to Him. But there is judgment for those who reject Him.

The Historical Books

The historical books include the next twelve books of the Bible (Joshua through Esther). They also tell a continuous story, beginning with Joshua leading the Hebrews into the land, their time in the land, their captivity out of the land and finally their restoration to the land. This covers a 1000-year period from about 1451-400 BC.

Joshua

Joshua took the charge from Moses and led the people into their land in about the year 1451 BC. God held back the Jordan River, allowing the people to cross it on dry land. He then gave the Hebrews a great victory, enabling them to take the city of Jericho without a conflict. Their next battle should have been easy, but they were defeated because of disobedience. *However, they repented and God gave them further victories, enabling them to possess the land.* The land was then divided among the tribes according to their inheritance. The book closes with Joshua's death. The people were faithful to God as long as Joshua and the elders who served with him were alive.

Jesus Christ is one greater than Joshua. If we will follow Him, He will lead us into a land of spiritual rest with God and give us victories over the enemies of our soul.

Judges

God told the Hebrews to annihilate all the pagans who were in the land. This was because they were so evil that God knew they would never turn from their sins, and if left in the land, they would contaminate the Hebrews with their wicked, idolatrous ways. But the Hebrews didn't obey God. And sure enough, they started worshiping the heathen gods and living immorally. Everyone did what was right in his own eyes. *It was the darkest period in the young nation's history.* God chose to use these pagan enemies of Israel as a means of disciplining the Hebrews to bring them to repentance. When the people were oppressed, they repented and cried out to God, and He sent judges to deliver them from their enemies. These judges were mostly military leaders. There were thirteen of these deliverers. And God ruled Israel through them. But the people soon forgot and went back to their sinful ways. This cycle continued throughout the book of Judges which covered the period of time from about 1400-1101 BC.

The judges and approximate years they served are as follows:

1. Othniel (forty years)   — 1400-1360 BC
2. Ehud (eighty years)   — 1360-1280
3. Shamgar (one year)   — 1280
4. Deborah (forty years)   — 1280-1240
5. Gideon (forty years)   — 1240-1200
6. Abimelech (three years)   — 1200-1197
7. Tola (twenty-three years)   — 1197-1174
8. Jair (twenty-two years)   — 1174-1152
9. Jephthah (six years)   — 1152-1146
10. Ibzan (eight years)   — 1146-1138
11. Elon (ten years)   — 1138-1128
12. Abdon (seven years)   — 1128-1121
13. Sampson (twenty years)   — 1121-1101

If a Christian does not effectively put away the sins of the flesh, he may backslide as the Hebrews did. God will discipline us to bring us to repentance. When we cry out to God for help, Jesus is always there to deliver us from our oppressions.

Ruth

Even during the dark period of the Judges, God was still able to save those who would seek Him with their whole hearts. This is the story of Ruth. She was a Moabitess who married a Hebrew who had come to Moab with his family. Her mother-in-law was Naomi. When Naomi's husband died, she desired to return to Israel. Her son, Ruth's husband, had also died. *Ruth returned to Israel with Naomi, promising to serve her and her God.* She married Boaz, who was her near kinsman through Naomi. Ruth became the great-grandmother of King David, and the ancestor of Jesus. The story of Ruth took place during the time of the Judges.

Jesus is our near kinsman. But we, like Ruth the Moabitess, are not His covenant people. So, He became one of us to save us from our sins. When we seek Him with our whole hearts, He will bring us out of our pagan lives, into the promised land of covenant blessings with God.

First Samuel

God raised up a young man named Samuel to guide the Hebrews during their transition from the time of the Judges to the time of the monarchy. *Samuel was a great prophet of God who kept the nation together during this difficult period.* The people trusted Samuel. When he grew old, he expected his sons to succeed him but they were wicked so the people wouldn't follow them. They demanded that Samuel appoint a king to govern them. Although this was not God's desire for the people, He directed Samuel to anoint Saul as the first king of Israel. Saul ruled from about 1096-1056 BC. But he was proud, and he disobeyed God. During Saul's rule, God chose David as His king to succeed Saul. Samuel anointed David while he was still a young shepherd boy. Saul became jealous of David, so that David had to live as an outlaw until Saul died. This book covers the period from about 1170 BC to 1056 BC.

Jesus is the true prophet of God. He only spoke the words the Father told Him to speak. We can trust His words to be true. And he told us to carry His words to all nations, guiding them out of their darkness and oppression to receive Him as their King.

Second Samuel

This book continues the story from First Samuel and is devoted entirely to the history of David's rule as king. *It gives the account of the battles David fought in order to unify Israel and make the country safe from its enemies.* It also relates the personal tragedies in David's life as he battled his own sins. Even though he often failed God, David sincerely wanted to please God. Therefore, God promised David that when He came to the earth as the Messiah, He would come through the seed of David. So that through the Messiah, David would have a son who would rule as king forever. (See 2 Sam. 7:12-16.) David's rule covered the period from about 1056-1016 BC.

First Kings

Just before David died, he appointed his son, Solomon, to

succeed him as king. Solomon was very wise and led Israel into her greatest period of glory. *His outstanding achievement was building the Temple in Jerusalem.* But he took many foreign wives who led him into worshiping their gods. In order to support their life style, Solomon oppressed the people with excessive taxes and forced labor. They revolted in 976 BC, and at Solomon's death, the kingdom was divided between north and south.

The northern kingdom was called Israel and consisted of ten tribes, and the capital was Samaria. The northern kingdom lasted about 255 years until it was conquered by Assyria in 721 BC. It had nineteen kings who were of nine different families. All of these kings were evil and led the people into idol worship which is why God brought them to defeat. *The most notable prophet in the book of First Kings is Elijah who warned the northern kingdom of God's coming judgments and challenged the prophets of Baal.*

The southern kingdom was called Judah and consisted of two tribes. Jerusalem was its capital. It lasted about 370 years until it was conquered by Babylon whose initial siege was in 606 BC. It was completely destroyed in 586 BC. The southern kingdom had nineteen kings and one queen, all from the line of David. Some were good and some were evil.

The book of First Kings covers the period of time from about 976-893 BC. It includes the rule of the first eight kings (Jereboam to Ahaziah) in the north and the first four kings (Rehoboam to Jehoshaphat) in the south.

Second Kings
This book continues the story of the divided kingdom where First Kings ends. The time period is about 893-586 BC. It begins with the history of the next eleven northern kings (Jehoram-Hoshea) and gives an account of the Assyrian conquest. *The outstanding prophet in this book is Elisha who succeeded Elijah as God's spokesman to the northern kingdom.* Then the story picks up with the southern kingdom and its next sixteen rulers (Jehoram-Zedekiah) down to the time when King Nebuchadnezzar of Babylon

conquered Judah, destroyed Jerusalem and the Temple, and took the people captive. Isaiah is mentioned as a prophet in the south.

The kings and approximate years they ruled are as follows:

Northern Kingdom (Israel)		Southern Kingdom (Judah)	
1. Jeroboam I	—976-954 BC	1. Rehoboam	—976-959 BC
2. Nadab	—954-953	2. Abijah	—959-956
3. Baasha	—953-930	3. Asa	—956-915
4. Elah	—930-929	4. Jehoshaphat	—915-893
5. Zimri	—929	5. Jehoram	—893-886
6. Omri	—929-918	6. Ahaziah	—886-885
7. Ahab	—918-898	7. Athaliah	—885-879
8. Ahaziah	—898-897	8. Joash	—879-840
9. Jehoram	—897-885	9. Amaziah	—840-811
10. Jehu	—885-857	10. Uzziah	—811-759
11. Jehoahaz	—857-841	11. Jotham	—759-743
12. Jehoash	—841-825	12. Ahaz	—743-727
13. Jeroboam II	—825-773	13. Hezekiah	—727-698
14. Zechariah	—773-772	14. Manasseh	—698-643
15. Shallum	—772	15. Amon	—643-640
16. Menahem	—772-762	16. Josiah	—640-609
17. Pekahiah	—762-760	17. Jehoahaz	—609
18. Pekah	—760-730	18. Jehoiakim	—609-597
19. Hoshea	—730-721	19. Jehoiachin	—597
		20. Zedekiah	—597

First Chronicles

The books of Samuel and Kings tell about the political history of Israel. The books of Chronicles repeats the story from a religious viewpoint. First Chronicles parallels First and Second Samuel. It provides important genealogical records as well as giving some details not mentioned in First and Second Samuel. The book ends with David's decree for building the Temple in Jerusalem.

Second Chronicles

This book parallels First and Second Kings but only reviews the history of the southern kingdom. *It begins with Solomon and ends with the fall of Jerusalem to Nebuchadnezzar.* However, the final two verses in the book mention a decree of King Cyrus of Persia. Persia conquered

Babylon in 536 BC. At that time, Cyrus issued a decree, allowing the Hebrews to return to their homeland and rebuild the Temple.

The books of Samuel, Kings and Chronicles all pointed the Hebrews toward the future when God himself would rule as king over His covenant people through the Lord Jesus Christ. His rule would be one of perfect justice in an everlasting kingdom of peace. We who know Jesus as our King have this same message to proclaim and are to live as kingly priests of the most high God

Ezra

Ezra continues the story with the decree of Cyrus. The Hebrews had been held captive in Babylon for seventy years from 606-536 BC. But now they were free to return home. *Ezra describes their return and the problems involved in rebuilding the Temple.* Zerubbabel led the first group of about 50,000 in 536 BC. Then, in 458 BC, Ezra led a second expedition of about 2,000. He was a faithful scribe who kept the religious records and helped preserve the laws of God, writing about them and teaching them to the people. Ezra covers the period of time from about 536-450 BC.

Jesus is our faithful scribe who has written our names in the Lamb's Book of Life. And we are to be as living epistles that others might see His laws written on our hearts.

Nehemiah

The Persian king during the time of Nehemiah was Artaxerxes. He appointed Nehemiah to be the governor of Judah. Then in 445 BC, he sent Nehemiah to Judah for the purpose of rebuilding the walls of Jerusalem. *The book describes Nehemiah's expedition to Jerusalem and the difficulties he encountered in carrying out the emperor's decree.* Nehemiah covers events that took place from about 445-410 BC.

Jesus is the restorer of the broken walls of our lives. He came to restore our souls when they have been cast down by sin and Satan. And we can also build up one another with the good news of Jesus Christ's restoring love and power.

Esther
The story in the book of Esther took place from about 485-465 BC, and this was between the expeditions of Zerubbabel and Ezra and Nehemiah. Esther was a beautiful Jewish maid who became queen to the Persian king, Ahasuerus. The king's prime minister, Haman, plotted to destroy all the Jews. *Esther's uncle, Mordecai, discovered the plot and asked Esther to risk her life by asking the king to save her people.*

Jesus is our Advocate who gave His life to save us from our sins. He reminds us that the greatest love a person can have is when he lays down his life to save another.

The Books of Poetry
The next five books in the Bible are the books of poetry. They are largely written in poetic style. These include all the books from Job, through the Song of Solomon. The continuous historical narrative in the Old Testament ends with these books; the books of poetry do not cover a specific period of time.

Job
Have you ever wondered why the righteous suffer? The book of Job answers this question. God said that Job was a righteous man. Today we would call him a Christian. *Yet, he suffered more than any man.* He lost his family, his material possessions, his friends and his health. His so-called friends falsely accused him. After a while, Job began to wonder himself and suggested that God was not dealing with him justly. However, he never lost his faith in his Redeemer who would justify him to his accusers.

Jesus is our Redeemer who will see us through our trials and sufferings. He will never leave us nor forsake us. And one day He will give us a new, glorified body so that we may be with Him and be like Him forever. Until then, the trials we go through increase our faith.

Psalms

This is the book of praise and prayer in the Bible. The Jews used it as their hymnbook. It includes worship, praise and prayers both on a national and personal level, expressing the deepest emotions of the human heart and soul. David wrote about half of the 150 psalms.

Jesus puts a new song in our hearts. When we know Him as our Lord and Savior, our hearts overflow with worship and praise to God. And our prayers are offered to God in His name.

Proverbs

This is the great book of wisdom. It includes a collection of wise sayings or teachings that can guide us in our everyday lives. Most of the Proverbs are credited to Solomon. This book emphasizes that real wisdom is knowing and walking with God.

Jesus is our wisdom. He presented himself as the way, the truth and the life. Through Him, we can know and walk in godly wisdom.

Ecclesiastes

Many people see no meaning and purpose in life. They try everything that the world can offer, yet they still feel empty on the inside. Life doesn't seem to make any sense. *This book describes this human view of life as it is without God.* Then it concludes with the observation that the only things in life that are worthwhile are to reverence God and to obey His commandments.

Jesus is our goal in life. He gives purpose to our lives and makes life meaningful. Therefore, He is our reason for living.

Song of Solomon

This book is a poem about the beauty and joy of marital love. It points us to Jesus, who, as our heavenly lover, has taken us to be His bride.

The Prophets

The last seventeen books in the Old Testament are the books of the prophets. A prophet is one who speaks for God. God raised up men to speak His words to the people and also to point them toward the future when the Messiah would come as the final and ultimate Word of God. Each prophet uniquely reveals something about the coming Messiah and when taken as a whole forms a complete picture of the Lord Jesus Christ.

The prophetic books were divided into two divisions. *These were the Major Prophets and the Minor Prophets.* This classification is based on the length of the books and not their value. The Major Prophets are the five longer books consisting of Isaiah through Daniel. The twelve Minor Prophets consist of the books from Hosea through Malachi. The prophetic books do not form a chronological historical narrative. Therefore, it is important to determine the time in which each prophet lived and to relate the historical setting to the events recorded in the historical books.

THE MAJOR PROPHETS

Isaiah

Isaiah prophesied in the southern kingdom of Judah from about the years 780-720 BC. This would cover the rule of four southern kings (Uzziah through Hezekiah). Assyria had conquered the northern kingdom and was threatening Judah. *Isaiah warned that the real threat was not Assyria but the nation's own sins. He called the nation back to God, and this spared them from an Assyrian conquest.* Isaiah's principle message about the coming Messiah was that He would be a suffering servant (Isa. 53). Likewise, all who live godly in Christ Jesus shall suffer persecution at the hands of the world.

Jeremiah

Jeremiah's prophetic ministry was in the southern kingdom from about the years 627-586 BC. This was the last forty years of the southern kingdom and included the rule of five kings (Josiah through Zedekiah). By the time of Jeremiah, the southern kingdom had once again turned its back on God. *Jeremiah had the unfortunate task of pronouncing judgment, but the people would not repent.* So, God allowed King Nebuchadnezzar of Babylon to conquer Judah in 606 BC, and to take the people captive. Jeremiah spoke of the Messiah as being the righteous branch of David (Jer. 23:5). We are saved from our sins through the righteousness of Jesus Christ.

Lamentations

Jeremiah wrote this collection of five poems as *he wept over the final destruction of Jerusalem* by the Babylonians in 586 BC. It portrays Jesus as the weeping prophet (Lam. 1-5). We too should weep over sin, destruction and death.

Ezekiel

When Nebuchadnezzar conquered Judah, he took the more prominent citizens captive and deported them to Babylon. Ezekiel was taken captive at this time, probably in 597 BC. Zedekiah was the king of Judah when this took place. Ezekiel became the prophet to the Hebrew people while they were in Babylon, and his ministry was from about 593-570 BC. *He spoke of the need for a new heart and prophesied doom against nations that come against Israel.* He saw Jesus as the glory of God (Ezek. 1). And God's glory is to be seen in His Church.

Daniel

Daniel was taken captive in the invasion in 606 BC. Whereas Ezekiel prophesied to the Hebrew people who were in captivity, Daniel prophesied to the Babylonian leaders. The Judean kings during this time were Jehoiakim, Jehoiachin and Zedekiah. *Daniel had a number of dreams about the future and spoke of Jesus as the rock that would destroy the heathen Gentile nations of the world* (Dan. 2). We can walk in victory over the world through Jesus Christ, the rock of our salvation.

THE MINOR PROPHETS

Hosea

Hosea was a prophet to the northern kingdom from about 770-730 BC, during the rule of the kings from Jeroboam II through Hosea. *His message was that Israel was like an unfaithful wife who needed to return to her husband.* Likewise, Israel needed to return to God. Hosea experienced this heartache through his own unfaithful wife. He wrote of Jesus as our heavenly lover who will never forsake us even though we may sometimes be unfaithful. But God has called us to be a pure and spotless bride for our Lord Jesus Christ.

Joel

The land of Palestine had been devastated by a terrifying invasion of locusts. Everything was destroyed. *Joel uses this to illustrate the coming destruction in the Day of the Lord.* But afterwards, God will bless those who turn to Him. It is believed that Joel prophesied in the southern kingdom from 878-870 BC, during the rule of Joash. He points us to Jesus as the one who will send the Holy Spirit to all who will receive Him (Joel 2:28, 29).

Amos

Amos preached to the northern kingdom in about the year 800 BC, during the rule of Jeroboam II. This was at a time of great wealth and prosperity. But there was injustice and oppression of the poor. *Amos called the people to social righteousness. He also rebuked them for their religious hypocrisy.* After prophesying doom, he looked forward to Jesus coming to restore the glory of the nation (Amos 9:11). As Christians, we should not be respectors of persons, but treat all with justice and mercy.

Obadiah

The book of Obadiah prophesies the destruction of the country of Edom. This is because Edom participated in the plunder of Jerusalem, possibly during the 606-586 BC invasion by Babylon. Zedekiah was king at the time.

Obadiah speaks of Jesus as the coming Savior (Obad. 1:17-21). The Christian message is that now is the acceptable year of the Lord, but judgment will come for those who plunder the things of God.

Jonah

God called Jonah to preach to the citizens of Nineveh, the capital city of Assyria. This was from about 824-804 BC, when Jereboam II was the king of Israel. Jonah ran from God and was swallowed by a great fish. But God delivered him and Jonah brought the message to Nineveh, and the people received it and were spared. Jonah pictures Jesus in His death and resurrection (Jon. 1:17). We can walk in that same resurrection power.

Micah

Micah prophesied in the southern kingdom along with Isaiah from about 775-740 BC. *His message was similiar to that of Amos regarding injustice and religious hypocrisy.* Micah saw Jesus as the ruler of all ages (Mic. 5:2). We are joint-heirs with Christ.

Nahum

Even though Nineveh repented through the preaching of Jonah, they later turned away from God. *God then raised up Nahum, in Judah, to prophesy against Nineveh.* The city was destroyed in 612 BC. Nahum preached from about 660-612 BC, during the rule of the kings from Manasseh through Josiah. To Nahum, Jesus was the avenger of his adversaries (Nah. 1:2). Christians are to leave vengeance with God.

Habakkuk

God raised up Habakkuk during the rule of King Jehoikim in about the year 609 BC. *He preached about the coming destruction of Judah at the hands of the Babylonians.* He was puzzled that God would use such an evil nation to punish Judah. He looked to Jesus as the God of his salvation (Hab. 3:19). All who call upon the name of the Lord Jesus shall be saved.

Zephaniah

Zephaniah preached in the southern kingdom during the rule of King Josiah in about 640 BC. *He warned of God's coming judgment at the hand of Babylon but also mentioned that God would restore them in due time.* He saw Jesus as the one who would come and live among them (Zeph. 3:17). Jesus is in our midst through the Holy Spirit who lives in each of us who are born again in Christ.

Haggai

Haggai, Zechariah and Malachi all prophesied in Judah after the Hebrews had come back to their land from Babylonian captivity. Haggai and Zechariah ministered at the same time (520 BC). Zerubbabel was the governor of Judah and was seeking to rebuild the Temple. But he was delayed in completing the task. *Haggai delivered a series of messages which encouraged the completion of the Temple.* He saw Jesus as the restorer of the kingdom of God (Hag. 2:7). We can help build the kingdom of God on planet earth.

Zechariah

Zechariah's ministry extended from 520-518 BC. *He was also a priest and along with Haggai encouraged Zerubbabel to complete rebuilding the Temple.* He also spoke about the coming of Jesus and the end of the age. To Zechariah, Jesus would be the priest on the throne (Zech. 6:13). All Christians are kings and priests of the most high God.

Malachi

This is the last book in the Old Testament. Malachi prophesied about the year 425 BC, while Nehemiah was governor. Once again the people were turning away from God. *Malachi rebuked them for their evil ways.* He spoke of Jesus as the one who would come with healing in His wings (Mal. 4:2). As Christians, we are to bring the healing love of Jesus Christ to an evil world.

Time of the Prophets

The approximate chronological appearance of the writing prophets is as follows:

Joel	—878-870 BC	—Southern Kingdom
Jonah	—824-804	—Northern Kingdom (Nineveh)
Amos	—810-800	—Northern Kingdom
Hosea	—770-730	—Northern Kingdom
Isaiah	—780-720	—Southern Kingdom
Micah	—775-740	—Southern Kingdom
Nahum	—660-612	—Southern Kingdom
Zephaniah	—640-608	—Southern Kingdom
Jeremiah	—627-586	—Southern Kingdom
Habakkuk	—609-586	—Southern Kingdom
Obadiah	—606-586	—Southern Kingdom
Daniel	—606-534	—In Babylonian Captivity
Ezekiel	—593-570	—In Babylonian Captivity
Haggai	—520-518	—Back in the Land
Zechariah	—520-518	—Back in the Land
Malachi	—425-400	—Back in the Land

Chapter 4—How the Old Testament Is Organized

Review Exercise 3

1. List the five major divisions of the Old Testament.

   a.   d.
   b.   e.
   c.

2. Under each major division, list the names of the books included in that division.

   a. _____   d. _____
   1.   1.
   2.   2.
   3.   3.
   4.   4.
   5.   5.

   b. _____   e. _____
   1.   1.
   2.   2.
   3.   3.
   4.   4.
   5.   5.
   6.   6.
   7.   7.
   8.   8.
   9.   9.
   10.   10.
   11.   11.
   12.   12.

   c. _____
   1.   3.   5.
   2.   4.

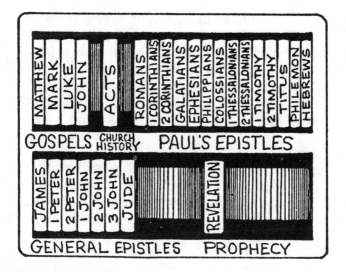

GOSPELS CHURCH HISTORY   PAUL'S EPISTLES

GENERAL EPISTLES   PROPHECY

5

How the New Testament Is Organized

In chapter three we saw that the Old Testament was written over a long period of time. But this is not true with the New Testament. As previously mentioned, the twenty-seven books in the New Testament were written from about 45 AD to 95 AD. Traditionally, the New Testament has been divided into the following four divisions: The Gospels, Church History, Epistles (Letters), Prophecy.

The Gospels

The word "gospel" means good news. The good news is that God has entered into an eternal covenant of love with us through the blood of the Lord Jesus Christ. *The Gospel books are about the only written record we have of the life and ministry of Jesus. And, as we read the gospels, we soon realize that they all tell the same story, but they tell it differently.* This is because each gospel writer is presenting a different view of Jesus, depending on to whom he is writing. But when we view all four gospels together, we see the complete portrait of Jesus which God wants us to have. The fact that the Gospels are different is further evidence that the writers were not just making up a story. If that had been the case, they would have made sure that they all told it exactly the same way.

Matthew

For centuries, the Jews had been waiting for their promised Messiah. In a way that they didn't quite understand, He would be God living among them and ruling over them as King of the Jews. There were many prophecies about His coming. One of the most important was that the Messiah would be the Son of David. As the Hebrews were subject to one Gentile power after another, they longed for the Messiah to come and establish His eternal kingdom of righteousness and peace. *Matthew, writing primarily to the Jews, presents Jesus as the Son of David and the Hebrew Messiah who came to establish the Kingdom of God.* Therefore, he begins his gospel record with the genealogy of Jesus, showing his readers that Jesus is a descendant of David and Abraham, with whom God originally made His covenant promise. And throughout his gospel, Matthew refers to the Old Testament by showing how it was fulfilled in the person and work of Jesus Christ. He does this more than any other gospel writer. In fact, he directly quotes from the Old Testament forty-seven times. Thus, Matthew's record proves that Jesus Christ was the King of the Jews.

Mark

Whereas Matthew wrote primarily to the Jews, Mark wrote to the Romans. The Romans ruled the world. They understood authority and power. So, Mark emphasizes this aspect of the life and ministry of Jesus. Matthew stressed what Jesus taught, while Mark stressed what Jesus did. Therefore, Mark's gospel record is fast-moving and packed with action. He doesn't stop to point out how Jesus was fulfilling the Old Testament, because this would mean nothing to the Romans. *Mark presents Jesus as the servant of Jehovah.* Since the ancestry of a servant is totally irrelevant, Mark sees no need to record the genealogy of Jesus. He lets Matthew record that while he starts with Jesus' baptism and quickly moves on to the action.

Luke
Even though Rome ruled the world through military power, Greece ruled the minds of men through philosophy. The Greeks were lovers of knowledge and sought to understand the nature and conduct of man. Luke wrote his gospel primarily to the Greeks. *Therefore, he presents Jesus as the perfect man. His gospel emphasizes the humanity of Jesus.* So, he begins by tracing Jesus' ancestry all the way back to Adam. And he gives more details about the human side of Jesus than do the other gospel writers. Luke emphasizes Jesus as the Son of man who came to seek and to save the lost.

John
Matthew wrote to the Jews, Mark to the Romans, Luke to the Greeks, but John wrote to the whole world. *The purpose of his gospel is to show the world that Jesus is the Son of God,* and that anyone who places faith in Him will receive eternal life. John emphasizes the deity of Jesus and traces His ancestry to God himself. Therefore, Jesus is God. To prove this point, John records many miracles that Jesus performed as signs which pointed the people to Jesus as the giver and sustainer of life.

CHURCH HISTORY
The next division of the New Testament is concerned with the early spread of Christianity. Luke records this for us in the book of Acts.

Acts
The gospels provide us with biographic sketches of the life

and ministry of Jesus. Jesus told His followers to spread the Gospel throughout the whole world, beginning at Jerusalem. *The book of Acts highlights the work of the Holy Spirit through man to carry out Jesus' command.* It begins with 120 of Jesus' followers timidly waiting for the anointing of the Holy Spirit, as Jesus had promised. Once they received His power, they boldly began to witness in the city of Jerusalem. But then persecution started with Stephen becoming the first to be killed. Many of Jesus' followers fled Jerusalem, taking the gospel with them wherever they went.

One of the persecutors was a man named Saul. But Saul had a vision of Jesus and was converted. He then became known as Paul, the apostle of Jesus Christ. Luke accompanied Paul on his missionary journeys. *In the last half of the book of Acts, he records the events which took place as Paul took the gospel to Europe, Asia, Rome, and through Rome, to the world.* Luke ends his account with Paul preaching the gospel from a Roman jail. In the book of Acts, Luke sees Jesus as the giver of the Holy Spirit.

THE EPISTLES (Letters)

The next and largest division of the New Testament contains the epistles. The epistles are twenty-one letters written by Paul, James, Peter, John and Jude. They are called epistles because of their formal style. Paul wrote thirteen of these epistles and possibly also the book of Hebrews. Although we do not know who wrote the book of Hebrews, I have included it with those written by Paul for the sake of convenience. *The main purpose of these letters is to interpret the gospel to those who have already believed it while showing how it applies to their lives.*

Paul's letters were written to a specific group or person and usually addressed one particular problem. Whereas, the other letters were written to a larger, more general audience and cover a variety of subjects. Therefore, they are usually set apart from Paul's letters and referred to as general epistles.

A. THE EPISTLES OF PAUL

Romans

Paul had a great desire to visit the Christians in Rome. But he would be delayed for a while, because he was attending to other matters. So, probably while in Corinth, he wrote them a letter to let them know he would be coming to see them as soon as possible. In this letter, Paul makes the fullest and most complete statements ever written concerning the great teachings of the Christian faith. *The theme of the letter is how a person becomes right with God.* Paul explains that we can only be right with God through faith in Jesus Christ. This is the act of justification where God credits the righteousness of Jesus Christ to our account. In Romans, Paul emphasizes Jesus.as our justifier.

First Corinthians

Corinth was a wealthy, cosmopolitan city in Greece. It was also very immoral. Paul went there in about 50 AD and preached the gospel for eighteen months. He then continued on, making his way to Ephesus where he wrote this letter. Word reached Paul that the new believers at Corinth were having problems. There were divisions and immorality among them. Some carried a letter to Paul containing questions from the church leaders. *These questions were about sex and marriage, proper conduct for Christians, church order, spiritual gifts and the resurrection of the dead.* Paul deals with the problems and answers their questions. He speaks of Jesus as the one who gives spiritual gifts to the Church for the purpose of mutual edification in love.

Second Corinthians

Some people in the church at Corinth did not receive Paul's first letter very well. They strongly criticized him and tried to excite the people against him. So, some months later, he had to write another letter. *He explains the necessity for his first letter and expresses gratitude for the good that it has worked in the believer.* He then encourages them to complete a commitment they had earlier made to take up a collection for the poor Christians in Jerusalem. Then he concludes his letter with a defense of his call from God as a true apostle of the Lord Jesus Christ.

Galatians

Paul's missionary journeys took him to the area called Galatia (modern Turkey), where he established various churches. However, after he left, some Jews came to the area and told the new believers that it was necessary for them to keep the Jewish laws, particularly circumcision, in order to be saved. *Paul heard about this dangerously false teaching and quickly sent a letter to the churches warning them against this form of legalism.* He begins by stating his apostolic authority and that his message of grace through faith came directly from God. He then states how legalism cannot save anyone nor make them holy. He concludes with a reminder that we have been freed from legalism by faith in Christ in order to serve one another in love. Paul emphasizes Jesus as the great liberator.

Ephesians

Ephesus was a great trade center situated on the Mediterranean coast of what is now the country of Turkey. It was also a center for the occult. Its main attraction was the great temple to the goddess Diana, which attracted many tourists. Paul went there in about 55 AD and preached for three years. In this book, he is writing back to them, about five years later, from a Roman prison. *His main theme is that Jesus Christ is the exalted one who has shared all spiritual blessings with His followers and made us to be one new creation in Him.* Therefore, we are to walk worthy of this high calling in love and unity, living a new life by being filled with the Holy Spirit and wearing the armor of God.

Philippians

Philippi was located in Greece and served as a major trade route and gateway between Asia and Europe. It was also a

Roman colony. Paul went there in about the year 55 AD and, through his preaching, the first European converts to Christianity were won. Paul and the Philippian Christians had a very warm relationship. So, when they learned that Paul was in jail, in Rome, they sent him an offering. *Paul wrote this letter to thank them for their help in his time of need.* He uses this as an opportunity to mention the need for unity and humbleness, steadfastness during tribulation, and to warn them against false teachers and remind them of the joy and peace that comes from living in harmony through Christ. He presents Jesus as our strength and joy.

Colossians

Colosse was situated in a beautiful valley about 100 miles inland from Ephesus. It seems that Paul passed through Colosse on his way to Ephesus. Some Colossians were converted in Ephesus through Paul's preaching. They carried the gospel back to Colosse, and a church was soon established. However, false teachers had confused the young believers. They were teaching that Jesus Christ, alone, was not sufficient for their salvation. In doing so, they denied His deity and work on the cross, substituting instead, angels and legalism. So, one of the leaders went to Rome where Paul was in jail to seek his help. *Paul writes this letter to establish the correct teaching concerning the person and work of Christ.* His basic theme is that Christ is the head of all things and that you are complete in Him. He then encourages the Colossian believers to apply this truth to their lives.

First Thessalonians

When Paul left Philippi, he made his way south to Thessalonica. In spite of great opposition, he preached the gospel and established a church. But he had to leave town because the Jews so violently opposed him. He then sent Timothy back to Thessalonica to encourage the new believers in their faith. Timothy rejoins Paul at Corinth where he writes this letter. He gives thanks for their commitment and reminds them of the example he was to them. *He then answers their questions about the Second Coming of Christ and encourages them to live pure, peaceable lives as they look for Christ to return.* This letter, along with Second Thessalonians, emphasizes Christ as the coming one.

Second Thessalonians

The Christians in Thessalonica still had problems about the return of Christ, and they were experiencing great persecution. So, Paul had to write them a second letter. *He encourages them in their persecution and explains that Christ will not come again until the antichrist comes first and there be a falling away from the true worship of God.* He then exhorts them to stand firm in their faith and live good, hard-working lives until Jesus comes.

First Timothy

Timothy had a Gentile father and a devout Jewish mother. His grandmother and mother taught him the Scriptures from an early age. When Paul came to his town and preached Jesus, Timothy was converted and began to accompany Paul on his missionary journeys. He eventually became the elder at the Church in Ephesus, where he received this letter. *Paul warns Timothy against false teachings, gives instructions regarding various pastoral considerations, and challenges Timothy to fight the good fight of faith.* In Timothy and Titus, Paul emphasizes Jesus as our faithful pastor.

Second Timothy

This is probably the last letter that Paul wrote before he died. *He encourages Timothy to faithfully preserve and pass on the Scriptures to others, to endure persecution, avoid foolish arguments and beware of the coming apostasy.*

Titus

Titus was a Gentile who was converted to Christ under

Paul's ministry. He then began to travel with Paul and, at the time of this writing, was the elder at the church in Crete. *Paul lists the qualifications for elders, warns against false teachers, gives advice regarding what to teach the various groups in the Church and speaks of the need for good works.*

Philemon

Philemon was a slave owner in Colosse. One of his slaves, Onesimus, ran away and found Paul in Rome. Onesimus was converted through Paul's witness. Paul then wrote his friend, Philemon to take Onesimus back. *He asks Philemon to receive Onesimus, not as a slave, but as a son.* He pictures Jesus Christ as our friend who has reconciled us to God so that we are no longer runaway slaves to sin but have become the children of God through faith in Him.

Hebrews

We are not sure who wrote the book of Hebrews. But the readers were Hebrew Christians who were tempted to live under the Old Covenant system, which would deny the finished work of Christ as the fulfillment of the Old Covenant. *The writer argues that Christ is superior to the Old Covenant system.* As the Son of God, He is superior to Moses, the prophets and to angels. As a High Priest who lives forever, He is superior to Aaron and his descendants. And His perfect sacrifice is greater than that of animals which must be offered again and again. Hebrews pictures Christ as the fulfillment of the Old Covenant. Those who have trusted in Him should remain faithful to Him and not go back to their old dead traditions.

B. THE GENERAL EPISTLES

James

James addresses his letters to the Jewish Christians who were living in the various Gentile nations; thus, it has a Jewish flavor. *Its primary emphasis is on practical Christian living.* James deals with a variety of subjects, including trials, temptation, receiving the word, prejudices, faith and works, use of the tongue, true wisdom, pride and humbleness, judging, presumption, patience and praying for the sick. He views Jesus as our great physician.

First Peter

Peter also addresses his letter to the Jewish Christians who were driven from Jerusalem and scattered to the Gentile nations. They were experiencing severe persecution and suffering for their faith in Jesus as the Jewish Messiah and Savior of the world. *Peter wrote this letter to encourage them in their difficulties, using Jesus as the supreme example of one who suffered unjustly.* He also appealed to them to live a life separate from the world. Peter's letters present Jesus as the chief cornerstone who holds our lives together.

Second Peter

In this letter, Peter warns the early Christians against false teachers who would lead their followers into immorality. He condemns these false teachers and mentions that God will not spare them in the Day of Judgment. He also warns against those who deny the return of Jesus Christ to planet earth, while encouraging the Christians to live separate from the world, awaiting Christ's return.

First John

John wrote this letter to confirm what he had already written in his gospel—that Jesus Christ is the Son of God. He shows that fellowship with God can only come through Jesus, whose blood cleanses us of all sin. He then encourages his readers to walk in true, loving fellowship with God and each other. He also warns them against false teachers who were denying that Jesus was God in the flesh, but that the believers' faith in Jesus Christ will enable them to overcome the world. John's letters view Jesus in terms of light and love.

Second John

In this second letter, John continues to appeal to the

believers to *love one another in truth,* and once again warns them against false teachers who were denying the deity of Jesus Christ.

Third John
John wrote this letter to a man named Gaius, commending him for helping fellow Christians. But he speaks against a man named Diotrephes who tried to exalt himself to a position of leadership.

Jude
Jude had intended to write about salvation through Jesus Christ. But he was prompted, instead, to encourage his readers to *contend for the faith against false teachers* who were perverting the gospel of the Lord Jesus. Jude's letter is very similar to Second Peter.

Prophecy
The last division of the New Testament is concerned with prophecy. In the book of Revelation, we see the Word of God and the plan of God completed.

The Revelation
John wrote the book of Revelation from the little island of Patmos, to which he had been banished because of his Christian witness. He begins by giving his vision of Jesus Christ in all of His glory, who gives John this *Revelation concerning future events.* Then John gives a panoramic view of Church history. Next, he provides information about the end-time tribulation period and the return of Jesus Christ. He concludes with a view of life on planet earth with Jesus ruling as King, and the new heaven and new earth.

NEW TESTAMENT CHRONOLOGY
The approximate time of the New Testament writings is as follows:

James	45 AD
1 Thessalonians	50

2 Thessalonians	51 AD
Galatians	52
1 Corinthians	54
2 Corinthians	55
Romans	56
Mark	60
Matthew	60
Philemon	60
Colossians	60
Ephesians	60
Philippians	60
Luke	63
Acts	63
Hebrews	65
1 Timothy	64
Titus	64
1 Peter	65
2 Timothy	66
2 Peter	68
Jude	69
John	85
1 John	90
2 John	90
3 John	90
Revelation	95

Review Exercise 4

1. List the four major divisions of the New Testament.

    a.
    b.
    c.
    d.

2. Under each major division, list the names of the books included in that division.

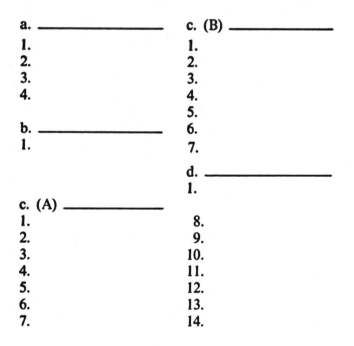

a. _____

1.
2.
3.
4.

b. _____

1.

c. (A) _____

1.
2.
3.
4.
5.
6.
7.

c. (B) _____

1.
2.
3.
4.
5.
6.
7.

d. _____

1.

8.
9.
10.
11.
12.
13.
14.

6

How We Got Our English Bible

Today, in the United States of America, we can go to almost any department store or bookstore and purchase a copy of the Bible in the English language. But this great blessing of having the Bible in our own language has not always been available to us. *There was a long period in history, when the Word of God was not in the language the people spoke.* Therefore, they could not read the Bible for themselves. This period of time has been rightly called the Dark Ages. But God gave us His Word so that all of us could read it for ourselves. Thus, He began to raise up men with the burden of translating the Bible into the English language. In this chapter, we're going to see how God went about doing this.

The chart at the end of the chapter will help you visualize how this took place. You will need to refer to it as we discuss the main highlights. First of all, you'll notice that there are two paths on the chart—Path A and Path B. The purpose of these two paths is to show that the New Testament in the English language Bible which we have today was actually translated from two different Greek texts. And there's a lot of debate among Bible scholars as to which Greek text is the real one that God inspired.

The Original Manuscripts

Let's begin with Path A and the original manuscripts. In chapter two, we learned that there are no original manuscripts of the Bible. However, I also pointed out that there are no original manuscripts of many other ancient writings that are never questioned concerning their authenticity and reliability. *We learned that the Bible has been more reliably preserved than any other ancient writing. Of course, it doesn't make sense that God would give us His Word and not preserve it for us.* He even promised to preserve it for us. Jesus said, "Heaven and earth shall pass away, but my words shall not pass away" (Matt. 24:35 KJV).

Ancient Copies, Translations, Church Fathers

Although God didn't leave us with any original manuscripts, He did the next best thing. *He left us with a considerable number of ancient copies, early translations and writings from the early church fathers.*

As mentioned in chapter two, there are approximately 5000 ancient, handwritten copies of the New Testament. And some of these copies are dated as early as 130 AD. Most of them don't contain the entire New Testament because a handwritten copy of the New Testament was too big to carry. So, the copies were made in sections. *The Dead Sea Scrolls verify the authenticity and reliability of the Old Testament.*

It didn't take long for people to begin to translate the Bible into different languages. Some of these, such as the Syriac and old Latin translations, date as early as 150 AD. And today, there are thousands of copies of various early translations.

Then there are the writings of the early church fathers. These men knew the apostles, and had access to the original New Testament manuscripts. In *Unger's Bible Handbook* (Moody Press, 1967), Merrill Unger says that more than 86,000 such quotations are known to us today.

We see, then, that God has clearly preserved His Word for us in the ancient copies, early translations and writings of the church fathers.

The English Translations

Now, let's see how the Bible was translated into English. We'll begin with Path B.

Origen

Path B begins with a Greek text produced by a man named Origen. Origen lived from 185-254 AD. Some Bible scholars believe that Origen was a great man of God. Others believe he was a heretic who taught views that were not properly Christian.

Origen was a philosopher. Many philosophers denied that Jesus Christ was God and that His death was necessary for our personal salvation. It seemed that Origen may have held to these views, even though he claimed to be a Christian. He became the head of a school in Alexandria, Egypt. This school tried to combine the teachings of Greek philosophy with the teachings of the Bible, in an attempt to harmonize the two. It was mixing Christianity with human wisdom and reason.

Origen produced a manuscript called the "Hexapla." This manuscript contained a translation of the Bible in Greek that many believe to be Origen's own "edited" version of the Bible. It appears that Origen may have made certain changes in his translation that would make the Bible more compatible with his own personal philosophy. If this is true, some of the changes in his translation would have to do with the person and work of Jesus Christ.

Eusebius

One of Origen's great admirers was a man named

Eusebius, who lived from 263-339 AD. He was the Bishop at Caesarea and became close friends with the Emperor Constantine. Constantine claimed to be a Christian in 312 AD. *And in 331 AD, he ordered his good friend, Eusebius, to make fifty copies of the Bible.* Naturally, Eusebius used Origen's supposed edited version as the basis for making his copies. The result was fifty copies of the Bible which may have reflected changes that Origen had made in producing his translation.

Jerome

Jerome was a great Bible scholar who lived from 345-420 AD. He was also a fan of Origen. In 383 AD, Pope Damasus commissioned Jerome to produce a new Latin translation of the Bible. As you can imagine, Jerome used the work of Origen and Eusebius to produce his Bible for the pope. *Jerome's Bible became the official Bible of the Roman Catholic Church.* It was called the Vulgate, meaning common Latin. However, it was based on Origen's supposed edited translation handed down by Eusebius. Therefore, certain parts of it may have been changed. Yet, the average person did not know this because he was uneducated and not able to read the Bible for himself. The religious leaders decided that they were the only ones who could properly understand the Bible, and they would interpret it for the people. And for 1000 years (382-1382 AD), the Word of God was kept from the world. People were told what it said, but they never had a chance to read it for themselves.

The Translations and the Men Behind Them

In the meantime, the predominant world language changed from Latin to English. And people began to be educated so they could read the Bible for themselves. God began to raise up men with a vision for getting the Bible into the language of the people. That language was English.

John Wycliffe

The first man God used in preparing an English translation was John Wycliffe. Wycliffe lived from 1329-1384 AD. He was a teacher and scholar at Oxford University in England, but his real burden was to translate the Bible from Latin into English, so the average person could read it.

This soon made Wycliffe public enemy number one of the religious leaders, who were still opposed to average people reading the Bible for themselves. *But under great persecution, Wycliffe published the first complete Bible in English in 1382 AD.* And he organized a group of traveling preachers to carry the Bibles into the countryside and teach the people the Word of God.

Wycliffe died of a stroke in 1384 AD. In 1482 AD, one hundred years after the completion of his work, the religious leaders dug up his bones and threw his ashes into the River Swift.

William Tyndale

As great as Wycliffe's accomplishment was, it had one major drawback. (See the chart at the end of the chapter.) It was translated from the Latin Vulgate rather than the original Hebrew and Greek languages in which the Bible was written. And that's not exactly what God had in mind.

God began to raise up other men to translate the Bible into English. The most famous of these was William Tyndale. He lived from 1492-1536 AD. Tyndale was also an Oxford scholar. And like Wycliffe, he too wanted to translate the Bible into English so that everybody could read it.

Tyndale was greatly influenced by a man named Erasmus. Erasmus was the greatest Greek scholar and teacher of his day. In 1516 AD, *Erasmus published the first Greek New Testament since the early manuscripts.* This was a major accomplishment and contribution toward understanding the Bible. The Greek text that Erasmus used as a basis for his New Testament edition was different from the one Jerome used in 382 AD.

Then in 1526 AD, Tyndale published the first New Testament in English that was translated directly from the original Greek language of the New Testament. He used the Greek text published by Erasmus as the basis for his translation. You'll see the importance of this as we continue.

Tyndale became public enemy number one of the religious leaders, who were still opposed to the average person reading the Bible for himself. He had to smuggle his Bibles to the people and was forced to stay in hiding for the rest of his life.

But God was finished with Tyndale. And in 1536 AD, the religious authorities caught up with him, condemned him for heresy, strangled him and burned him at the stake. His last words were, "Lord, open the eyes of the King of England." Well, God heard Tyndale's prayer because in that same year, King Henry VIII gave permission to circulate the Coverdale Bible which was a revision of Tyndale's Bible.

The Coverdale Bible

A rapid succession of English translations soon followed Tyndale's. Next, came the Coverdale Bible published by Miles Coverdale in 1535 AD. And, as just mentioned, the Coverdale Bible was basically a revision of Tyndale's Bible. *It was the first complete English Bible, containing both the Old Testament and the New Testament, translated from the original Hebrew and Greek languages.* It was also the first English Bible to circulate without official hindrance from the political and religious leaders. This opened the door for numerous other translations.

The Matthew Bible

The Matthew Bible was published next in 1537 AD. It was a revision of the Tyndale-Coverdale Bible. It was compiled by a man named *John Rogers,* who, for reasons of safety, wrote using the pen name of Thomas Matthew.

The Great Bible

In 1539 AD, the government of England asked Miles Coverdale to prepare another revision of the Bible. This revision was to be based on the Matthew Bible. It was called the Great Bible because of its size which was sixteen-and-a-half inches by eleven inches. *The Great Bible was the first authorized English Bible.* This means that the Word of God in English had come out from the underground. Copies of the Great Bible were placed in churches and chained to stands so that people would not steal them as they gathered around to read for themselves. Much to the discouragement of the preachers, the people would stand around and read this Bible rather than listening to the sermons.

The Geneva Bible

But things turned sour for the translators. The government reversed its tolerant attitude and once again began persecuting translators and anyone caught with an English Bible. A few years later, Queen Mary I attempted to burn all the English translations as well as the translators. Under her rule, 300 translators and their followers were burned at the stake, including John Rogers. But Coverdale escaped to Geneva, Switzerland, where he published the Geneva Bible in 1560 AD.

The Geneva Bible became the Bible of the people. It was very popular with the average citizen, but it was not popular with religious leaders. The Great Bible was the "official church Bible," but all the people were ignoring it and reading the Geneva Bible. The religious leaders couldn't allow that situation to continue, so they set out to publish a Bible that would replace them both.

The Bishop's Bible

The result was the Bishop's Bible, published in 1568 AD. *It was called the Bishop's Bible because the revising translators were bishops.* The Bishop's Bible never completely replaced the Geneva Bible in the hearts of the people, but it did set the stage for the next revision which was the King James Version.

The Rheims-Douay Bible

Before the King James Version was published, the Roman

Catholic hierarchy, finally with great reluctance, published a Bible in the English language. This was called the Rheims-Douay Bible. The New Testament was completed in 1582 AD, and the Old Testament was completed in 1610 AD. *Of course, it was translated from Jerome's Latin Vulgate which came from Eusebius's revision of Origen's supposed edited version.*

The King James Version

When Queen Elizabeth I died in 1603 AD, James I became King of England. Some of his new subjects requested another revision of the Bible. James, wanting to please them, agreed. In 1607 AD, he appointed forty-seven scholars to begin work on the new version. It was to be a revision of the Bishop's Bible, and it was to be translated in such a way that it could be used in public services and be read privately at home by the average citizen. The King James Version of the Bible was completed in 1611 AD. *You will notice that the King James Bible and all the versions leading up to it, were translated from the same Greek text of the New Testament. This was the Greek text of Erasmus. The Roman Catholic version was translated from the Greek text of Origen.*

Introducing Wescott and Hort

Over the years, the English language began to change. And some of the words in the King James Version no longer meant what they did in the 1600s. So, around 1875 AD, there was a movement to update the King James Version by replacing the words which had changed in meaning with more modern words.

This was a good idea, but it doesn't appear that it worked out exactly that way. *Instead of simply revising the King James Version, a completely different Bible was published. Yet, it was presented to the Christian world as though it was merely an updated revision of the King James Version.*

Here's what many Bible historians believe happened. Two men, B.F. Wescott (1825-1901 AD) and F.J.A. Hort (1828-1892 AD), were among the leading religious scholars of their day. And it seems that they wanted to replace the Greek text of Erasmus, on which the King James Version was based, with the Greek text of Origen. They had been working together for many years to bring about this change. Perhaps they saw this as their opportunity. So, when a committee was formed to revise the King James Version, they greatly influenced the work of the committee members and promoted their Greek text as being superior to the Greek text of Erasmus. They convinced the committee to keep their work secret for the next twenty years until their work was complete. Finally, they published their version of the New Testament in 1881 AD, and the complete Bible in 1885 AD.

This new Bible was called the English Revised Version. And it was promoted to the Christian world as a modern revision of the King James Version with just the old words updated. However, it seems that it may have been more than just a revision. This is because the committee relied heavily on the Greek text produced by Wescott and Hort, rather than the Greek text of Erasmus. *We need to be aware that all Bible versions that have been published after the King James Version use a different Greek text for the New Testament than did the King James Version and its predecessors.*

You've probably noticed in your modern Bibles many footnotes which say something like, "Other manuscripts read. . . ." Then the footnote will give a reading that is different from the King James Version. The reason is because all of the modern Bibles use a different Greek text than the one used by the translators of the King James Version. This essentially makes them a different Bible, although God can use any of them to touch our hearts with His grace.

A New King James Version

The problem we have today with the King James Version of the Bible is the same problem that existed in the late 1800s. The English language has changed. We don't use words in the same way they were used during the time of King James. Therefore, we still need a revised or updated

King James Version. In 1979, Thomas Nelson Publishers produced a New Testament using the same Greek text as that employed by the translators of the King James Version. The language usage has been updated with modern words replacing older words wherever meanings have changed. *This publication is called The New King James Bible (NKJ).* In 1982, the Old Testament was completed. The result is an updated revision of the King James Version of the Bible based on the Greek text of Erasmus.

We see that God has raised up men who gave their lives in order that we might be able to read, study and understand the Word of God for ourselves. This is what we will be learning in the remaining chapters of this book.

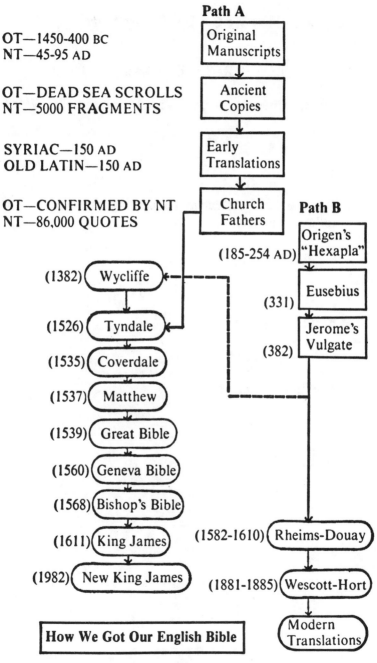

Path A

OT—1450-400 BC
NT—45-95 AD

OT—DEAD SEA SCROLLS
NT—5000 FRAGMENTS

SYRIAC—150 AD
OLD LATIN—150 AD

OT—CONFIRMED BY NT
NT—86,000 QUOTES

Original Manuscripts

Ancient Copies

Early Translations

Church Fathers

Path B

(185-254 AD) Origen's "Hexapla"

(1382) Wycliffe

(331) Eusebius

(1526) Tyndale

(382) Jerome's Vulgate

(1535) Coverdale

(1537) Matthew

(1539) Great Bible

(1560) Geneva Bible

(1568) Bishop's Bible

(1611) King James

(1582-1610) Rheims-Douay

(1982) New King James

(1881-1885) Wescott-Hort

Modern Translations

How We Got Our English Bible

75

Chapter 6—How We Got Our English Bible

Review Exercise 5

1. List the three ways God has used to preserve His Word.

    a.
    b.
    c.

2. Write a brief statement concerning the work of the following people:

    a. Origen—

    b. John Wycliffe—

    c. William Tyndale—

    d. Wescott and Hort—

7

How to Get Into the Bible

God has given us the Bible as a written revelation of who He is and what He expects of us. God has done this because it is His desire for us to come to know Him and learn to walk with Him. The result is that we can live abundant Christian lives. But this only happens in our lives as we give ourselves to study God's Word. Paul said to Timothy, "Study to shew thyself approved unto God, a workman that needeth not to be ashamed, rightly dividing the word of truth" (2 Tim. 2:15, KJV).

A Book You Can Understand

God desires that we study His Word. This is His will for us. *And God has written the Bible so simply that every Christian can understand it.* It certainly doesn't make sense that God would go to all the trouble to write a book, yet write it in such a complex manner that only a few scholars could understand it. Certain parts of the Bible are more difficult than others, however. And these require a great deal of study. But the basic teachings of Christianity are written so simply that any Christian can understand them. To help us, Jesus has given the Holy Spirit, who is the real Bible teacher.

Yes, God wants us to study His Word. He has written it simply enough for us to understand it. And He has even promised to teach it to us. You can have confidence in God's ability to help you understand the Bible.

Best Seller, but Least Read

We all know that many Christians do not study the Bible as they should. I've observed two reasons for this. *The first reason is basic laziness.* The spirit is willing but the flesh is weak. When a person first becomes a Christian, everybody tells him that he needs to study the Bible. Often, the individual begins with great excitement and expectation. But soon he learns that there aren't going to be any thunderbolts from heaven. This studying-the-Bible business is going to take work. It's going to take discipline. It's going to require a commitment. When people realize this they begin to lose some of their zeal. They begin to make up excuses as to why they can't study the Bible. And they become satisfied with letting the preacher tell them what it means on Sunday morning.

For this reason, it is important for us to have a clear statement of the problem: "Studying the Bible is hard work and we don't have the discipline to do it." Therefore, as a starting point, we must confess this need to God and ask for His help. And since we know that God desires for us to study His Word, we know that He will help us.

The second reason why many Christians don't study the Bible as they should is because they don't know how to study God's Word. They don't have a good system for Bible study. They read a little here and a little there, but they don't understand the whole of the Bible nor how its parts are related. It's very important, therefore, to know how to study the Bible.

78

Keys to Effective Bible Study

There are two keys to effective Bible study. The first key is that Bible study must be *systematic.* A system is an orderly means of doing something. For example, an effective housewife has a system she follows in buying her groceries. It begins with her shopping list. Then, when she goes to the grocery story, she knows exactly what she needs. If she usually buys at a particular market, she knows where everything is located. So, when she makes her list, she groups the items together according to their locations in the store. When I go to the store, on the other hand, I don't know what we need at home, nor where many items are located. It always seems as if there are endless varieties of the same items. Often, I get very confused and give up. Now, this is the problem many people have when they study the Bible. They don't have an orderly method for studying the Bible, so they get confused and give up.

The second key to effective Bible study is that it must be *consistent.* We must do it regularly. This means at least fifteen minutes a day. We must have a good system of Bible study and we must stick with it.

In this chapter, I hope to encourage you to make the commitment that is necessary to study God's Word effectively. God will help you if you are willing. And He promises to bless you as a result. We are going to discuss five of these blessings.

In subsequent chapters, we will see a plan that will help you to study the Bible in a systematic and consistent manner.

Blessings of Bible Study

Blessing 1—You Will Become a Strong Christian.

The first blessing of Bible study is that it helps you to become a strong Christian. Peter wrote, "As newborn babes, desire the sincere milk of the word, that ye may grow thereby" (1 Pet. 2:2, KJV).

In order for a little baby to be strong and healthy, he must have his milk. There's no substitute for milk. And just having the milk around the house and hearing about how good it is won't help the baby. The baby must drink the milk for himself. And he must drink it every day. If he doesn't drink it every day, he will get weak and sick. But if he does consume his milk, he will grow and become strong and healthy.

It's the same way with Christians. Peter says the Bible is our spiritual milk. And we must feed on it in order to grow strong spiritually and become mature Christians. *There is no substitute for feeding on God's Word.* There is no other way for the Christian to grow. Just having the Bible around the house doesn't help us. Nor does it help us if we only hear others talking about how good it is. We must feed on it ourselves.

I've noticed that some Christians seem to spend all of their time going to religious gatherings to hear someone else talk about the Word of God. They try to feed themselves on the testimonies of others. These people find that they have to keep going to meeting after meeting in order to increase their faith. They know there is something lacking in their own Christian experience, so they seek to grow through other people's testimonies. However, when it doesn't work out that way, these people begin to think there's something wrong with them. They become confused, frustrated and discouraged.

The problem is that such a person is trying to grow as a result of another person's testimony and experience with God. But you cannot feed on the things God has done in the life of someone else. The same problem applies to reading books and listening to tapes as replacements for your own personal Bible study. Other Christians can get too occupied with church programs and "working for the Lord." The Bible says, "So then faith comes by hearing, and hearing by the word of God" (Rom. 10:17, NKJ).

We need to hear the Word of God for ourselves. And we need to hear it every day or else we will become weak and sick spiritually. *But if we will feed on God's Word each day, God will strengthen us spiritually and we will grow to be strong, healthy, mature Christians.* That's a pretty good blessing, isn't it?

Blessing 2—*You Will Be Cleansed of Sin.*

The second blessing of Bible study is that it will help cleanse you of sin. King David learned this and wrote, "Thy word have I hid in mine heart, that I might not sin against thee" (Ps. 119:11, KJV). Jesus said, "Now ye are clean through the word which I have spoken unto you" (John 15:3, KJV). Paul says that Christians are cleansed by the "washing of water by the word" (See Eph. 5:26).

How does God use the Bible to cleanse us of sin? When you go about your daily chores, you get tired, sweaty and dirty. You come home after work, look into the mirror and see that you need a bath. So, you take your bath and scrub real good. When you finish bathing you are cleaner than you were before.

God uses the Bible in a similar manner. As we walk every day in the world, we get spiritually dirty—we sin. And when we look into the Bible, we see our sin. *The Bible is God's divine mirror that shows us His perfections and reveals our sins.* At the same time, the Bible is also like a tub of hot water that the Holy Spirit uses to cleanse us. When we get into the Word of God, the Holy Spirit scrubs us down real good. After this spiritual bath, we are much cleaner than we were beforehand. So, the same Word of God that reveals our sins, also washes them away by the power of the Holy Spirit.

Blessing 3—*You Will Bear Fruit.*

The third blessing of Bible study is that it will help you to bear fruit. Jesus said, "Abide in Me, and I in you. As the branch cannot bear fruit of itself, unless it abides in the vine, neither can you, unless you abide in Me. I am the vine, you are the branches. He who abides in Me, and I in him, bears much fruit; for without Me you can do nothing" (John 15:4-5 NKJ).

The branch receives its life from the vine. The vine produces the fruit. The branch only bears it. However, the branch is only able to bear the fruit as it abides in the vine.

We Christians cannot produce fruit ourselves. We are only fruit bearers. It is the fruit of the Spirit, not our fruit. Jesus says that we bear this fruit by abiding in Him. We abide in Him when we allow the Holy Spirit to control our lives and produce His fruit in us. The fruit of the Spirit which we will bear is love, joy, peace, longsuffering, kindness, goodness, faithfulness, gentleness, and self-control. (See Gal. 5:22-23.) *The Holy Spirit produces this fruit in us as we meditate on the Word of God.*

The Bible says it this way, "Blessed is the man that walketh not in the counsel of the ungodly, nor standeth in the way of sinners, nor sitteth in the seat of the scornful. But his delight is in the law of the Lord; and in his law doth he meditate day and night. And he shall be like a tree planted by the rivers of water, that bringeth forth his fruit in his season; his leaf also shall not wither; and whatsoever he doeth shall prosper" (Ps. 1:1-3, KJV).

Blessing 4—You Will Learn How to Pray.

The fourth blessing of Bible study is that it will help you learn how to pray. Jesus said, "If you abide in me, and my words abide in you, ask whatever you will, and it shall be done for you" (John 15:7, RSV).

Jesus' words abide in us as we study the Bible and allow His words to take root in our hearts. And the words of God express the will of God. We learn how to pray as we know the will of God. We learn the will of God through Bible study. And when we know that we're praying according to God's will, we can have confidence that God is going to say "yes" to our prayers.

John put it in these words, "Now this is the confidence that we have in Him, that if we ask anything according to His will, He hears us. And if we know that He hears us, whatever we ask, we know that we have the petitions that we have asked of Him" (1 John 5:14-15, NKJ).

You can start by studying the prayers in the Bible and making them your own personal prayers. You can be confident that God will answer these prayers because you will be praying His own words back to Him. Some prayers you can study and make your own are found in Matt. 6:9-13; Eph. 1:17-19; Eph. 3:14-19; Phil. 1:9-11; Col. 1:9-12.

Blessing 5—You Will Know God's Will.

The fifth blessing of Bible study is that it will help you know God's will and receive divine guidance. One of the reasons why God gave us the Bible was to enable us to know His will. We all need guidance. We all have many decisions to make along life's journey. How do we know what to do? How do we know what is right? How do we know God's will?

We know God's will through personal Bible study. Psalms 119:105 says, "Thy word is a lamp unto my feet, and a light unto my path" (KJV). God has given us principles in the Bible to guide our lives. Perhaps 90 percent of all the guidance we will ever need is found in these principles. God's Word will guide us and help us to make the right decisions. But only if we know what it says.

How to Hear From God

The purpose of studying the Bible is to hear from God. But in order to hear from God, we must have a proper heart attitude. God will not teach us unless we have a heart attitude that is prepared to receive from Him. Four heart attitudes are necessary to understand the Bible and hear from God.

Attitude 1—A New Heart

The first requirement to understand the Bible is that you must have a new heart, or as Jesus said, "You must be born again" (See John 3:1-7). God spoke through Ezekiel and said, "A new heart also will I give you, and a new spirit will I put within you; and I will take away the stony heart out of your flesh, and I will give you an heart of flesh" (Ezek. 36:26, KJV).

A Christian is someone who possesses Christ. When we ask Christ to come into our hearts, He comes to live in us through the Holy Spirit. The Holy Spirit is the one who teaches us and guides us into all truth. *So obviously, if a person does not have the Holy Spirit, he cannot understand the Bible.* He can acquire much knowledge about the Bible, its history, and its people and even have an appreciation for the teachings of Jesus. But he cannot understand the spiritual truths in the Bible unless he is born again.

Paul described this necessary heart attitude, "But we know about these things because God has sent his Spirit to tell us, and his Spirit searches out and shows us all of God's deepest secrets. No one can really know what anyone else is thinking, or what he is really like, except that person himself. And no one can know God's thoughts except God's own Spirit. And God has actually given us his spirit (not the world's spirit) to tell us about the wonderful free gifts of grace and blessing that God has given us. In telling you about these gifts we have even used the very words given to us by the Holy Spirit, not words that we as men might choose. So we use the Holy Spirit's words to explain the Holy Spirit's facts. But the man who isn't a Christian can't understand and can't accept these thoughts from God, which the Holy Spirit teaches us. They sound foolish to him, because only those who have the Holy Spirit within them can understand what the Holy Spirit means. Others just can't take it in" (1 Cor. 2:10-14, TLB).

Attitude 2—A Humble Heart

God will not teach the proud. He reveals himself to the humble in heart. James understood this well and said, ". . . God resists the proud, but gives grace to the humble" (James 4:6, NKJ). *A humble person is one who realizes he doesn't know it all and is open to further instruction. He has a teachable spirit.*

The apostle Peter had been a very proud man. He thought he had all the answers. He wouldn't listen to others. But after three years of walking with Jesus, he learned how to receive instruction. This once proud man wrote, ". . . Yes, all of you be submissive to one another, and be clothed with humility, for God resists the proud, but gives grace to the humble" (1 Pet. 5:5, NKJ).

Sometimes God teaches us directly from His Word on an individual basis. However, most of the time He teaches us indirectly through our pastors, teachers, and Christian friends. We must be willing to receive the Word of God through whatever means or human vessels God chooses to use to bring His Word to us.

Attitude 3—An Obedient Heart

God will give understanding and enlightenment only to those who obey Him. He does not tell people things if He knows they aren't going to do them. He does not teach truths to those who will not receive them. But if we walk in the light that God has given us, then He will give us more light. *If we don't walk in the light that He has already given us, then He won't give us more light.*

James wrote, "But be ye doers of the word, and not hearers only, deceiving your own selves" (James 1:22, KJV). We can deceive ourselves with a belief that we are going to hear from God when we are not willing to obey what He wants to tell us. For example, many times in our prayers, we ask for guidance. But God knows that if He did give us guidance, we wouldn't receive it anyway. So He withholds His guidance until we come to the point of being willing to do what He wants. Then He gives us His word of guidance in a way that we can understand it.

Attitude 4—A Hungry Heart

God teaches us whenever we are hungry for Him to teach us. When Peter wrote that we should desire the milk of the word, he meant that we should *intently crave it*—like a baby crying for his milk.

Digging for the Gold

It's easy to find pretty shells as you walk along the beach. All you have to do is bend over and pick them up. It doesn't require much effort because the shells are laying on the surface. However, finding gold is entirely different. Gold lies below the surface. You have to dig and work to find it. *Understanding the Bible is not like picking up shells. It is like digging for the gold. The great truths of God lie below the surface. You must dig to find them.* Solomon wrote, "If you seek it like silver and search for it as for hidden treasures; then you will understand the fear of the Lord and find the knowledge of God" (Prov. 2:4-5, RSV).

Hearing from God must be the most important thing in your life. As Jesus said, "Blessed are they which do hunger and thirst after righteousness: for they shall be filled" (Matt. 5:6, KJV). When we hunger to hear from God and approach Him with a proper heart attitude, the Holy Spirit will take the words off the pages of the Bible and make them come alive in our hearts. For man does not live by bread alone but by every word that proceeds out of the mouth of God.

So, yes, God wants us to study His Word. He has given us teachers to help us understand it. But He has also given us the Holy Spirit so we can study for ourselves. *When people are hungry, you can either feed them or teach them how to feed themselves. It is a good thing to feed them. But it is even better to teach them how to feed themselves. In these next chapters, we are going to learn how to feed ourselves.*

Review Exercise 6

1. State the two main keys to effective Bible study.

   a.
   b.

2. List five blessings God promises to those who study His word.

   a.
   b.
   c.
   d.
   e.

3. List four heart attitudes which are necessary to understand the Bible and to properly hear from God.

   a.
   b.
   c.
   d.

8

How to Read the Bible

In the last chapter, I mentioned that the key to effective Bible study is that it must be systematic and consistent. This means that you must have some kind of orderly routine for studying the Bible. And you must stick to it faithfully. In these next chapters, we'll discuss, in detail, a plan that will help you establish this routine. And I pray you will ask God for help in committing yourself to it. God will bless you in return.

Difference Between Reading and Studying

The reason we study the Bible is to learn more of God and to apply what we have learned to our lives. But we must know how to learn. *The learning process involves two steps. The first step is reading. The second step is studying.* Many people read the Bible but few actually study it. Yet, there is a great difference between reading and studying.

Reading is simply oberving what is written for the purpose of getting information. *So, we read to be informed.* When we read, we often do not concern ourselves with the meaning behind what we are reading. This means that we do not stop to try to understand all the details. We are simply obtaining information. After we have obtained certain information through reading, we then go back and study that information to gain understanding.

Studying is meditating on what is written for the purpose of getting understanding. To meditate means to think, dwell on and ponder. That takes time—and work and discipline. It is much more involved than just reading.

People often ask me what a particular statement in the Bible means. Since I have read the Bible many times, I have some information or knowledge about the statement. But I may not have had an opportunity to study that particular statement. If that is the case, I have to say, "I know what it says but I'm not sure what it means. I'll have to study it first for understanding and then give you my view."

A lot of Christians try to give their views of the Scriptures out of information rather than understanding. They've read a certain passage but they have not studied it. This is one reason why people often have different opinions about the meaning of a particular passage in the Bible. But until we have actually studied the passage in question, we should not try to give our view on what we think it means. As Jesus said, ". . . Can the blind lead the blind? shall they not both fall into the ditch" (Luke 6:39, KJV). We can fall into the ditch of error and confusion through opinions that are based on information rather than understanding.

In light of this, we realize that reading and studying are not the same. *We read to get information; we study to get understanding.* Both are necessary in learning the Bible. In this chapter, we are going to learn how to read the Bible.

How to Read the Bible

How you read the Bible is important. The following six essentials will help make your Bible reading time most productive.

90

1. Begin at the Beginning

The first essential is to begin at the beginning. By this I mean you should start at Genesis and keep reading until you get to the end of Revelation. *It is important that you read the whole Bible all the way through before you begin to personally study its parts.* Now here is the reason for this. The central story of the Bible is found throughout all sixty-six books. Therefore, if you don't have an overview of the entire story, you will not be able to understand its parts properly in your personal Bible study. In this regard, we read the Bible like we do any other book. We start at the beginning.

It seems that we usually tell people to begin reading their Bible in the New Testament. The Gospel of John or the book of 1 John are often mentioned as starting points. The reason for this is that most people get bogged down in the Old Testament and never make it to the New Testament. They start out well in Genesis and Exodus but they get stuck in Leviticus. Many get discouraged and give up. To overcome this problem we often tell people to begin their reading in the New Testament.

There are two main reasons why people get bogged down in their reading of the Old Testament. One is that they have tried to read the Old Testament in an old English version which contains language usages that are unfamiliar to them. It is difficult for most of us to consistently read the Old Testament over a period of time in the King James English. The other reason why people get bogged down reading the Old Testament is that they become entangled trying to understand all of the details rather than simply reading it for the purpose of getting information.

2. Read in a Modern English Version

If you will read the Old Testament in a modern version and not stop to study the details as you read, you won't have any trouble making it to the New Testament. Remember that you are reading to get information, not to study the meaning behind what you are reading. *Therefore, I believe you will gain the most information in the shortest period of time if you will read the Bible in a modern English language version.*

There are a number of modern English language versions of the Bible. Perhaps the most popular Bible for reading is the Living Bible (TLB). It is easy to read because it is written in simple, everyday language. You can read it rapidly without getting bogged down. However, the Living Bible is a paraphrase rather than a direct translation. Therefore, it is most helpful as a reading Bible rather than a study Bible. Depending on which modern English version you use, you may need one Bible for reading and another for studying. If your Bible is an easy-to-ready translation, you can use it for both reading and studying.

3. Read Every Day

It is very important that we read the Bible every day. We feed our bodies several times each day. This is necessary to keep our bodies strong and healthy. If we did not eat on a regular basis, we would soon become weak and puny. It is the same with our spirits. We must feed our spirits with the Word of God on a regular basis. *Many people are weak spiritually because they neglect their spiritual food.* Have you noticed that many times we eat even though we may not feel like eating and are not hungry. This is because we eat out of habit. It is part of our daily routine. Likewise, we must feed our spirits with the Word of God even though we may not feel like it. In other words, *reading the Bible should become a habit for us that we automatically include in our daily routine.*

How much time should we spend each day reading the Bible? Of course that depends on your desire. But the very minimum is fifteen minutes. That is not much time at all, is it? We spend a lot more time than that doing many other things. Therefore, fifteen minutes of your day devoted to God's Word is certainly not a demanding requirement. Let me tell you what you can accomplish in that fifteen minutes.

In just fifteen minutes a day, you can read through the entire Bible in one year. Here is how. There are 1,189 chapters in the Bible—929 in the Old Testament and 260 in the New Testament. Some of these chapters are rather long while others are relatively short. But the average chapter length is about twenty-five verses. In a modern language Bible, a person with average reading skills can read a complete chapter in about five minutes. Therefore, you can read about three chapters in fifteen minutes. If you will read three chapters Monday through Saturday and five chapters on Sunday, you will finish reading the Old Testament in the middle of September and complete the New Testament at the end of November.

4. Read at a Regular Time

It is very important to set aside a regular, established time for reading each day. I believe your best time for reading is in *the morning*. There are two reasons for this. First of all, our minds are more alert in the morning than at night. That, of course, is after you have had your shower and morning coffee and gotten the sleep out of your eyes. Another reason for reading in the morning is that you will receive spiritual strength before you have to face that day.

So this means planning your morning wake-up routine so that you will have fifteen minutes to read the Bible before going to work. If you work at night and sleep during the day, then set your reading time according to that schedule. If you have special problems so that this does not work for you, then set some other time. The main objective is to read at least fifteen minutes at the same time every day.

5. Read at a Regular Place

It is also helpful to set aside a regular, established place where you will read each day. You need one particular place where you can go for your reading time. This should be a place where you can be alone with God with few distractions. It would be best if you had a little desk at which you could sit. But if you don't have a desk, use the kitchen table. Remember though, if you sit at the kitchen table, make sure there is no food on it or you will spend your fifteen minutes feeding your body instead of your spirit. *So, try to find a regular place and read at that same place, at the same time, every day.*

6. Mark as You Read

It is also helpful to mark your Bible as you read. Have you ever read something and found an hour later that you couldn't remember what you read? One reason why this happens is that we have trouble concentrating or focusing our thoughts on what we are reading. Our minds tend to wander in other directions. So often we read *at* something, but we don't really *read* it. We see the words but our mind does not take in what we are reading. Therefore, our reading does not do us much good.

However, if you are prepared to mark as you read, you will give more attention to what you are reading. This will help you to concentrate and keep your mind from wandering. It's okay to mark in your Bible. There's nothing sacred about the pages. It would help you to get several marking pens of the felt-tip variety and to mark those passages that stand out in your mind as you read. This will help you spot them easier when you reread the passage at a later date. Make sure the marks are light enough that they do not show through the page. You may have to try several types of markers to find the one that is best suited for your particular Bible.

In this chapter, you have learned a systematic and consistent reading plan that will help you to get through the whole Bible within less than a year. In the next chapter, you will discover how to meditate on what you have read. This will prepare you to study the Bible properly and to understand its related parts. God bless you as you continue in your reading.

Chapter 8—How to Read the Bible

Review Exercise 7

1. Explain the difference between reading and studying.

   a. Reading:

   b. Studying:

2. List the six essentials for effective Bible reading. Briefly mention in your own words why each is important.

   a.

   b.

   c.

   d.

   e.

   f.

9

How to Meditate on the Scriptures

As important as it is to read the Bible, this in itself is not enough to get God's Word into our hearts, or spirits. We must also learn to *meditate* on God's Word.

God told Joshua that meditating on His Word was the key to prosperity and success. He put it this way, "This book of the law shall not depart out of your mouth, but you shall meditate on it day and night, that you may be careful to do according to all that is written in it; for then you shall make your way prosperous, and then you shall have good success" (Josh. 1:8, RSV).

David added the following words of encouragement. "Blessed is the man who walks not in the counsel of the wicked, nor stands in the way of sinners, nor sits in the seat of scoffers; but his delight is in the law of the Lord, and on his law he meditates day and night. He is like a tree planted by streams of water, that yields its fruit in its season, and its leaf does not wither. In all that he does, he prospers" (Ps. 1:1-3, RSV).

God desires for us to meditate on His Word. Our ministers frequently challenge us to do so. We know that we should. But the question so many Christians ask is: *How do we meditate on God's Word?* Have you ever asked yourself that question? Let's now discover the answer.

The Meditation Process

In the previous chapter, I mentioned that the word meditate means to think, dwell on and ponder. It may be compared to the process of *rumination*. Rumination is what a cow does when it chews its cud. You see, a cow has two stomachs. After the cow chews on some grass, it swallows the grass into its first stomach. Then the cow lies down and thinks about how good that grass tasted. When the cow gets hungry again, it brings the grass up and chews on it some more. But this time the grass tastes differently. The cow then swallows the grass again, brings it up, chews on it and repeats the process until it has gotten the "full flavor" of that grass. Finally, the cow completely digests the grass into its second stomach where it becomes part of the cow's very being.

In a similar way, we chew on God's Word. But instead of sending it to a "first stomach," *we put it in our minds.* We then think about that particular Scripture passage again and again over a period of time. We think about it when we wake up in the morning. We consciously dwell on it throughout the day. We go to sleep contemplating its meaning. During our sleep, it resides in our subconscious minds so that, even while we're sleeping, God's Word is active in our minds.

This process is repeated until we get the full flavor (meaning) of the Scriptures. This happens when the Holy Spirit gives us divine illumination and spiritual understanding. At that point, we digest the Scriptures into our spirits where the message becomes part of our very being. This is how God's Word gets from our heads into our hearts.

Jeremiah had this process in mind when he said to God,

"Your words are what sustain me; they are food to my hungry soul" (Jer. 15:16, TLB).

Jesus said it this way, "Man shall not live by bread alone but by every word that proceeds out of the mouth of God" (Matt. 4:4, NKJ).

In order for God's Word to sustain us, it must get down into our second stomach (heart or spirit). It must become part of us. Just having it in our heads is not good enough. The words of Christ must dwell in us (Col. 3:16).

This is what the Psalmist meant when he said, "Thy word have I hid in mine heart, that I might not sin against thee" (Ps. 119:11, KJV).

Steps to Meaningful Meditation

Meditation (the process of getting God's Word from our heads to our hearts) involves *four steps.* Each of these steps represents a different way of contemplating a particular Scripture passage. These four steps are: *memorizing, visualizing, emphasizing and personalizing.*

Let's now learn how to apply these four steps using a familiar passage from Paul's letter to the Philippians. He wrote, "I can do all things through Christ who strengthens me" (Phil. 4:13, NKJ).

Step 1—Memorize

The first step in meditating on this verse is to *memorize* it. This is necessary because we must be able to recall the verse to our minds. Let's try it together. Before preceeding to step two, say this verse a number of times until you can repeat it from memory. You probably already know this verse. But give it a try anyway. The first time you say it, speak slowly, making sure that you have every word correct. And be sure to say the verse aloud. This will slow you down a bit and help you to concentrate.

Now repeat the verse, saying it a little faster each time until you are talking at a normal speed. Once you have it memorized, you will be able to think about it throughout the day. Are you ready for step two?

Step 2—Visualize

The second step is to *visualize* the scene in the Bible in which the particular Scripture passage was written. Your objective in visualizing the scene is to put yourself into the very lives of the participants involved in the story. You will want to so identify with them that you feel what they felt, think what they thought, etc. This means you must learn as much as you can about the circumstances surrounding the story.

Concerning our Philippians verse, we know that Paul wrote this letter from a Roman jail. It was the Roman custom to chain the prisoner to a guard. We can reasonably assume this was the case with Paul. Can you picture yourself in Paul's shoes, in a Roman jail, chained to a prison guard twenty-four hours a day?

But instead of literal chains, you may be chained to the prison guard of this world system—Satan! You may be chained to sin! You may be chained to the fear of death! Yet, "You can do all things through Christ who strengthens you." By God's power, you can overcome the chains of Satan. You can break the hold of sin. You've been set free from the fear of death. Hallelujah! Jesus has set you free!

Can you see that in your spirit? Can you picture yourself as an overcomer in Christ? I'm sure you can. And to reinforce that picture, you now want to emphasize every word in the verse.

Step 3—Emphasize

You *emphasize* a Scripture passage by reading it through a number of times, focusing your thoughts on a different word each time. For example, Philippians 4:13 would be emphasized as follows:

"I can do all things through Christ who strengthens me."

"I CAN do all things through Christ who strengthens me."

"I can DO all things through Christ who strengthens me."

"I can do ALL things through Christ who strengthens me."

"I can do all THINGS through Christ who strengthens me."

"I can do all things THROUGH Christ who strengthens me."

"I can do all things through CHRIST who strengthens me."

"I can do all things through Christ WHO strengthens me."

"I can do all things through Christ who STRENGTHENS me."

"I can do all things through Christ who strengthens ME."

Let's try it together. Say the verse aloud; then stop and think about the word you emphasized. What is the word? What does the word mean? What does the word mean to you? Repeat this process until you have emphasized each word in the verse. As you do this, you will begin to realize that the difference between "I" and "me" in this verse is CHRIST! He makes the difference in your life. All things are possible through Him.

Step 4—Personalize

Now you're ready for the last step which is to *personalize* the verse. The purpose of personalizing the verse is to make it a reality in your own life. You do this either by saying the verse in the first person singular (I or me), or by saying your own name in place of the nouns or pronouns used by the Scriptures. For the Philippians verse, for example, you would say your own name in place of "I" or "me." Try it and see how it makes the meaning of the verse become much more personal.

Chapter 9—How to Meditate on the Scriptures

Review Exercise 8

1. Explain in your own words what it means to meditate.

2. Describe the process of meditation.

3. List the four steps involved in meditation, and briefly mention why each is important.

   a.

   b.

   c.

   d.

10

How to Study a Book in the Bible

In our last two chapters, we discovered that there is a big difference between reading and meditating. Once we have gathered information through reading, we then go back and meditate on what we have read. Meditation leads us into Bible study. There are two basic ways to study the Bible. One is to study book by book, and the other is to approach your study according to topic or subject. In this chapter we are going to cover how to study a book in the Bible.

How to Study a Book in the Bible

We have mentioned that there are sixty-six books in the Bible. Which one should we study initially? *I have found it helpful to begin with a short book in the New Testament.* A short book is one that has six chapters or less. There are seventeen short books in the New Testament, so you have a big choice. If you begin with a short book, you can study it in a short period of time. This will greatly encourage you as you see yourself making progress. When you finish studying your first book, pick another short one. And before you know it, you will have gained great confidence and made considerable progress. I suggest you start with either Colossians or Philippians; both are only four chapters long. Now, how do we go about it?

Three Phases of a Book Study

There are *three phases* involved in studying a book in the Bible: (1) Book Survey (2) Book Analysis (3) Book Summary. We are going to learn what each of these are and how to accomplish them. There are three Bible Book Analysis Forms at the end of this chapter that will help you in your study. We will be referring to these forms in this chapter. Notice that there is one form for each phase involved in the book study. There is also a complete sample book analysis using the book of Philemon as an example.

One of the main concerns we have in Bible study is to be certain we know what questions we need to be asking ourselves as we study. *If we don't know what questions to be asking, we certainly won't be getting the right answers.* These forms, then, simply list the questions you need to be asking yourself for each phase in your book study. They will guide you to the answers you should have in order to understand the book properly. Then the Holy Spirit will open your mind to understand the answers.

It would be helpful if you purchased an inexpensive notebook for the purpose of writing your notes. You could then copy these forms in your notebook, leaving appropriate spaces between questions for recording your answers. In this way, you would have all your Bible study notes organized in one place.

Phase 1—Book Survey

The first phase is the Book Survey. *The purpose of the Book Survey is to get an overview of the entire book.* Each book of the Bible was written for a specific purpose and has

104

an overall theme. The Book Survey will help you to determine this overall theme. Of course, the main purpose of every book is to teach us about Jesus Christ. Each book teaches some main point about Jesus. But that main point is unique to each particular book. Each book also addresses unique problems and circumstances which must be determined within the setting of the book.

How to Do a Book Survey

We do a Book Survey by simply reading the book. *You should read the whole book in one sitting.* This is easy for you to do with a short book. For example, you can easily read the whole book of Colossians or Philippians in ten to twenty minutes.

Now you are not normally going to find the main theme of the book the first time through. *Therefore, you have to keep reading it a number of times until it jumps out at you.* It would help if you were to read aloud. When you read aloud, it helps you to read more slowly, and when you read more slowly, you can better concentrate and think about what you are reading.

At this point you are not concerned with details. You are just looking for the general emphasis of the book. So, don't try to stop and analyze what you are reading or you will get bogged down. Just read!

The Book Survey Form

The Book Survey Form is divided into five sections. These are: Major Characters, Historical Setting, Purpose, Theme, and General Outline. As you read, you complete the questions under each section.

1. Major Characters.

This section will help you determine the major characters involved in the book. It is important to know who wrote the book and to whom he was writing. Any other major characters should be noted also. Then you should try to determine their relationship to each other.

2. Historical Setting.

It is important to know the historical setting of the book. You will want to find out when and where the book was written, and in what circumstances or condition it was written. It would be helpful to know the historical, cultural and geographic environment as well.

3. Purpose.

This section will help you determine why the book was written. You will want to pick out the major problems that are mentioned either directly or indirectly and what solutions are given to solve these problems.

4. Theme.

You must know the major theme of the book in order to understand why the book was written and the reason for the way it was written. You can discover this by looking for recurring ideas, phrases and words. This will help you locate the key verses in the book and its main teaching about Jesus Christ.

5. General Outline.

You should also make a general skeletal outline of the book. You will be able to fill in the details of the outline as your study progresses. Some Bibles have book outlines at the beginning of each book. They are very good and helpful. However, try to make your own first; then compare yours with others.

Phase 2—Book Analysis

The second phase is the Book Analysis. *The purpose of the Book Analysis is to understand the book and its related parts.*

How to Do a Book Analysis

Bible books are divided into chapters. Each chapter is further divided into paragraphs. A paragraph normally contains information about one subject or unit of thought.

What you actually want to study are the subject paragraphs within each chapter. This means that, as you read a chapter, you will want to try to identify the paragraphs that are in the chapter. Then determine the subject of the paragraph and isolate it by deciding which verses make up the paragraph. Give each subject paragraph a name. This will give you an outline of each chapter by subject paragraph within the chapter. *You then study each subject paragraph by answering the questions on the Book Analysis Form.* Sometimes a subject paragraph may continue on into the next chapter. If so, continue on with it. Don't stop just because you have come to the next chapter.

The Book Analysis Form
The Book Analysis Form is organized by chapter number and subject paragraph. *There are three basic questions you will want to answer for each subject paragraph.* These are divided into the following three sections: What does the passage say? What does the passage mean? What does the passage mean to me?

A. What Does the Passage Say? (Observation)
The first question you will want to answer about the subject paragraph concerns what it says. This is called "observing the passage." As you observe the passage, be looking for the main subject, points, phrases and words. And, make sure you understand what the main words mean.

Most of us want to know what God means before we know what He says. So, we hurriedly read through a passage and try to interpret it. This usually results in a wrong interpretation. But when you observe a passage, don't try to interpret it. First, become thoroughly familiar with what it says.

B. What Does the Passage Mean? (Interpretation)
Once you know what a passage says, you can then "interpret what it means." There is only one correct interpretation for the passage. The questions on the form

will help you to properly interpret the passage in order to receive the enlightenment of the Holy Spirit. The guiding principle is to interpret the passage within its context. You do this by considering the passage in relationship to its subject paragraph, chapter, book, testament and overall Bible view of the subject. Then you put yourself in the shoes of the main characters, considering the historical setting determined from your Book Survey.

C. What Does the Passage Mean to Me? (Application)

You are now ready to determine what the passage means to you personally. This is called "applying the passage." Although there is only one correct interpretation, there are many applications. The application is the Word of God to you personally. This may involve: an example to follow, a sin to avoid, a command to obey, a promise to claim, an action to take, an attitude to adopt or a principle or truth to learn. When you complete your Book Analysis, you will have a thorough understanding of the book and know how to apply it to your life. You will have heard from God.

Phase 3—Book Summary

You are now ready to complete your study in the third phase which is the Book Summary. The purpose of the Book Summary is to *consolidate* what you have learned in your study.

How to Do a Book Summary

You do a Book Summary by simply summarizing what you have learned. This involves reviewing your study notes and highlighting the main points and key elements of your study.

The Book Summary Form

The Book Summary Form is divided into four sections: Purpose and Theme, Final Outline, Main Subjects, and Final Application.

1. Purpose and Theme.

In this section, you state, in as few words as possible, the main purpose and theme of the book.

2. Final Outline.

Earlier in your Book Survey, you made a general outline of the book. You filled in the details during your Book Analysis. Now you are going to make a final, detailed outline incorporating all that you have learned.

3. Main Subjects.

In this section, you list by name the main subject paragraphs in each chapter. Then list the main points made in each subject paragraph.

4. Final Application.

By the time you complete your study, you will have discovered a number of applications of the Word of God to your own life. You now want to list these all together so that they will be clear in your mind and easy to review in the future. You should also make note of any false teachings exposed by the book.

Planning Your Time

In this lesson we have looked at a systematic plan for studying Bible books. It is a general plan that you can use to study any book in the Bible. And you can spend whatever time you are able to spend or that you desire to spend. Obviously, the more time you spend, the more you will learn. However, if your time really is limited, this plan will help you learn the most in the least amount of time. I suggest that you spend thirty minutes each evening. *This means that you are reading for fifteen minutes in the morning and studying for thirty minutes in the evening.* Forty-five minutes a day is really not very much time. But you can make tremendous progress if you will follow this systematic reading and study plan, and stick with it, using the learning principles I have suggested.

Sample Book Analysis

The sample book analysis which follows is based on Paul's letter to Philemon. I chose this book as an example because it is short, only one chapter long, and it should be easy for you to look over. You may want to study the book of Philemon for the purpose of using it to gain some experience and practice in studying Bible books. Then compare your results with the example that is given. You could do this on your own or as a project in a Bible study group. If you are in a Bible study group, share your results with the other members. Then, after group discussion, look over the following example. This will help you develop needed confidence to tackle a longer Bible book in your personal studies. The complete book of Philemon is quoted, followed by blank forms for your personal notes and the completed example.

BIBLE BOOK ANALYSIS FORM

PHASE 1—BOOK SURVEY

1. Major Characters
   A. Who is the author of the book?
   B. To whom is he writing?
   C. Other major characters?
   D. What is their relationship to each other?

2. Historical Setting
   A. When was the book written?
   B. Where was the book written?
   C. In what circumstances was it written?
   D. What is the historical setting?
   E. What is the cultural setting?
   F. What is the geographic setting?

3. Purpose
   A. Why was the book written?
   B. What are the major problems?
   C. What solutions are presented?

4. Theme
   A. What is the major theme of the book?
   B. What are the recurring ideas?
   C. What are the key verses, words?
   D. What is the main teaching about Jesus Christ?

5. General Outline
   A. What is the general outline of the book?

BIBLE BOOK ANALYSIS FORM

PHASE 2—BOOK ANALYSIS

A. **Chapter Number:**
  1. **Paragraph (subject and verses)**
    A. **What does the passage say (observation)?**
      1. What is the main subject?
      2. What are the main points?
      3. What are the main phrases?
      4. What are the main words?
      5. What do the main words mean?

    B. **What does the passage mean (interpretation)?**
      1. What is the paragraph context?
      2. What is the chapter context?
      3. What is the book context?
      4. What is the testament context?
      5. What is the Bible context?
      6. What would the reader understand the point to be?
      7. What would we understand the point to be?

    C. **What does the passage mean to me (application)?**
       Is there:
      1. An example to follow?
      2. A sin to avoid?
      3. A command to obey?
      4. A promise to claim?
      5. An action to take?
      6. An attitude to adopt?
      7. A principle or truth to learn?

BIBLE BOOK ANALYSIS FORM

PHASE 3—BOOK SUMMARY

1. Purpose and Theme
   A. What is the main purpose of the book?
   B. What is the main theme of the book?

2. Final Outline
   A. What is the final outline of the book?

3. Main Subjects
   A. What are the main subjects in each chapter?
   B. What main point is made in each subject?

4. Final Application
   A. How can I apply each main point to my life?
   B. What false teaching does the book expose?

SAMPLE BOOK ANALYSIS

PHILEMON

1 Paul, a prisoner of Jesus Christ, and Timothy our brother, unto Philemon our dearly beloved, and fellow-labourer,

2 And to our beloved Apphia, and Archippus our fellow-soldier, and to the church in thy house:

3 Grace to you, and peace, from God our Father and the Lord Jesus Christ.

4 I thank my God, making mention of thee always in my prayers,

5 Hearing of thy love and faith, which thou hast toward the Lord Jesus, and toward all saints;

6 That the communication of thy faith may become effectual by the acknowledging of every good thing which is in you in Christ Jesus.

7 For we have great joy and consolation in thy love, because the bowels of the saints are refreshed by thee, brother.

8 Wherefore, though I might be much bold in Christ to enjoin thee that which is convenient,

9 Yet for love's sake I rather beseech thee, being such an one as Paul the aged, and now also a prisoner of Jesus Christ.

10 I beseech thee for my son Onesimus, whom I have begotten in my bonds:

11 Which in time past was to thee unprofitable, but now profitable to thee and to me:

12 Whom I have sent again: thou therefore receive him, that is, mine own bowels:

13 Whom I would have retained with me, that in thy stead he might have ministered unto me in the bonds of the gospel:

14 But without thy mind would I do nothing; that thy benefit should not be as it were of necessity, but willingly.

15 For perhaps he therefore departed for a season, that thou shouldest receive him forever;

16 Not now as a servant, but above a servant, a brother beloved, specially to me, but how much more unto thee, both in the flesh, and in the Lord?

17 If thou count me therefore a partner, receive him as myself.

18 If he hath wronged thee, or oweth thee ought, put that on mine account;

19 I Paul have written it with mine own hand, I will repay it: albeit I do not say to thee how thou owest unto me even thine own self besides.

20 Yea, brother, let me have joy of thee in the Lord: refresh my bowels in the Lord.

21 Having confidence in thy obedience I wrote unto thee, knowing that thou wilt also do more than I say.

22 But withal prepare me also a lodging: for I trust that through your prayers I shall be given unto you.

23 There salute thee Epaphras, my fellowprisoner in Christ Jesus;

24 Marcus, Aristarchus, Demas, Lucas, my fellow-labourers.

25 The grace of our Lord Jesus Christ be with your spirit. Amen. (KJV)

PHASE 1—BOOK SURVEY

1. **Major Characters**
   A. Who is the author of the book?

   B. To whom is he writing?

   C. Other major characters?

   D. What is their relationship to each other?

2. **Historical Setting**
   A. When was the book written?

   B. Where was the book written?

   C. In what circumstance was the book written?

   D. What is the historical setting?

   E. What is the cultural setting?

   F. What is the geographic setting?

3. Purpose

A. Why was the book written?

B. What are the major problems?

C. What solutions are presented?

4. Theme

A. What is the major theme of the book?

B. What are the recurring ideas?

C. What are the key verses, words?

D. What is the main teaching about Jesus Christ?

5. **General Outline**
   A. What is the general outline of the book?

PHASE 2—BOOK ANALYSIS

A. Chapter Number: (1)
    1. Paragraph (Greeting—verses 1-3)
        A. What does the passage say? (Observation)
        1. What is the main subject?

        2. What are the main points?

        3. What are the main phrases?

        4. What are the main words?

        5. What do the main words mean?

        B. What does the passage mean? (Interpretation)
        1. What is the paragraph context?

2. What is the chapter context?

3. What is the book context?

4. What is the testament context?

5. What is the Bible context?

6. What would the reader understand the point to be?

7. What would we understand the point to be?

C. What does the passage mean to me? (Application)

2. **Paragraph** (Thanksgiving—verses 4-7)
    A. What does the passage say? (Observation)
    1. What is the main subject?

    2. What are the main points?

3. What are the main phrases?

4. What are the main words?

5. What do the main words mean?

B. What does the passage mean? (Interpretation)
1. What is the paragraph context?

2. What is the chapter context?

3. What is the book context?

4. What is the testament context?

5. What is the Bible context?

6. What would the reader understand the point to be?

7. What would we understand the point to be?

C. What does the passage mean to me? (Application)

3. **Paragraph** (Appeal for Onesimus—verses 8-21)
    A. What does the passage say? (Observation)
    1. What is the main subject?

    2. What are the main points?

3. What are the main phrases?

4. What are the main words?

5. What do the main words mean?

B. What does the passage mean? (Interpretation)
1. What is the paragraph context?

2. What is the chapter context?

3. What is the book context?

4. What is the testament context?

5. What is the Bible context?

6. What would the reader understand the point to be?

7. What would we understand the point to be?

C. What does the passage mean to me? (Application)

4. **Paragraph** (Closing—verses 22-25)
   A. What does the passage say? (Observation)
   1. What is the main subject?

   2. What are the main points?

3. What are the main phrases?

4. What are the main words?

5. What do the main words mean?

B. What does the passage mean? (Interpretation)
1. What is the paragraph context?

2. What is the chapter context?

3. What is the book context?

4. What is the testament context?

5. What is the Bible context?

6. What would the reader understand the point to be?

7. What would we understand the point to be?

C. What does the passage mean to me? (Application)

PHASE 3—BOOK SUMMARY

1. Purpose and Theme

   A. What is the main purpose of the book?

   B. What is the main theme of the book?

2. Final Outline

   A. What is the final outline of the book?

3. Main Subjects
   A. What are the main subjects in each chapter?

   B. What main point is made in each subject?

4. Final Application
   A. How can I apply each point to my life?

   B. What false teaching does the book expose?

PHASE 1—BOOK SURVEY

1. **Major Characters**
   A. Who is the author of the book? (Paul.)

   B. To whom is he writing? (Philemon.)

   C. Other major characters? (Onesimus.)

   D. What is their relationship to each other?
      1. Philemon—Slave owner living in Colosse.
                 —Master of Onesimus.
                 —Church meets in his house.
      2. Onesimus—Philemon's runaway slave.
      3. Paul—Philemon's friend and spiritual father who is instrumental in Onesimus' conversion in Rome.

2. **Historical Setting**
   A. When was the book written? (60 AD)

   B. Where was the book written? (From Rome)

   C. In what circumstances was it written? (Paul was in jail.)

   D. What is the historical setting?
      1. Roman Empire ruled the world.
      2. City of Rome—a haven for runaway slaves.

   E. What is the cultural setting?
      1. Slavery—the normal social order.
      2. Roman Empire built with slave labor.
      3. About six million slaves in Roman Empire.
      4. Runaway slaves could appeal to master's friend to represent them before the master.

5. If friend was a co-partner, the master might adopt the runaway slave into his own family.

F. What is the geographic setting?
It was about 2000 miles from Colosse to Rome.

3. Purpose
A. Why was the book written?
Paul writes Philemon, interceding on behalf of Onesimus.

B. What are the major problems?
How to deal with a runaway slave in a just, but merciful way.

How to avoid the wrath of Rome by advocating the abolition of slavery.

C. What solutions are presented?
Paul asks Philemon to take Onesimus back, not as a runaway slave, but as a brother in Christ.

Paul also asks Philemon to receive Onesimus as he would receive Paul and adopt him into his own family.

4. Theme
A. What is the major theme of the book?
Paul deals with the problem of how justice and mercy can both be served without compromising either.

B. What are the recurring ideas?
1. Paul is the co-partner with Philemon, while at the same time the friend of Onesimus.
2. Paul is the mediator who represents Onesimus.
3. Philemon should forgive Onesimus and receive him as he would receive Paul.
4. Paul is to be charged with Onesimus' debt.

C. What are the key verses, words?
1. Key verses (8-21).
2. Key words.
   a. Receive him.
   b. Willingly.
   c. Servant—brother.
   d. Partner—receive him as myself.
   e. Put his wrong to my account.
   f. I will repay it.

D. What is the main teaching about Jesus Christ?
Jesus is God who willingly laid aside His glory to become one of us in order to pay our sin debt. He was co-partner with God while, at the same time, becoming our friend. All of our sins were put to His account as He became sin for us. God receives us as He receives Jesus. Therefore, we are no longer runaway slaves to sin and the devil, but have become the children of God by faith in Jesus Christ.

5. General Outline
A. What is the general outline of the book?
1. Greeting—verses 1-3.
2. Thanksgiving—verses 4-7.
3. Appeal for Onesimus—verses 8-21.
4. Closing—verses 22-25.

PHASE 2—BOOK ANALYSIS

A. Chapter Number: (1)
  1. Paragraph (Greeting—verses 1-3)
   1. What is the main subject?
      Paul greets Philemon, his family and the church which meets in Philemon's house.

   2. What are the main points?
      To lovingly greet all those concerned with the problem.

   3. What are the main phrases?
      a. Prisoner of Jesus Christ.
      b. Dearly beloved.
      c. Church in thy house.

   4. What are the main words?
      a. Prisoner.
      b. Dearly beloved.
      c. Fellowlabourer.
      d. Fellowsoldier
      e. Grace.
      f. Peace.

   5. What do the main words mean?
      a. Prisoner—a person bound as a captive.
      b. Dearly beloved—a term of endearment.
      c. Fellowlabourer—sharing in the work.
      d. Fellowsoldier—sharing in the fight.
      e. Grace—favor you cannot earn.
      f. Peace—harmony and rest.

B. What does the passage mean? (Interpretation)
1. What is the paragraph context?
   Paul's introductory greeting.

132

2. What is the chapter context?
   The beginning of the chapter and introduction to the letter.

3. What is the book context?
   This greeting is to *all* concerned.

4. What is the testament context?
   Paul often uses this type of greeting in his letters.

5. What is the Bible context?
   Grace is a word with meaning to the Greeks.

   Peace is a word with meaning to the Hebrews.

6. What would the reader understand the point to be?
   Paul was greeting all of the saints with love.

7. What would we understand the point to be?
   Paul was greeting all the saints with love.

C. **What does the passage mean to me? (Application)**
1. An example to follow?
   We should greet one another in love, including all the saints of God.

---

2. **Paragraph** (Thanksgiving—verses 4-7)
   A. **What does the passage say? (Observation)**
   1. What is the main subject?
      Paul thanks God for the love and faith the believers have expressed towards Jesus Christ and each other and that others will see it in them and respond to it.

   2. What are the main points?
      That through the demonstration of their faith

and love, the Colossian Christians would live as
the salt of the earth and the light of the world,
having a powerful and effective witness in the
community.

3. What are the main phrases?
   a. I thank my God.
   b. Hearing of thy love and faith.
   c. Toward all saints.
   d. Communication of thy faith become effectual.

4. What are the main words?
   a. Thank God.
   b. Love.
   c. Faith.
   d. Lord Jesus Christ and all saints.
   e. Communication.
   f. Effectual.

5. What do the main words mean?
   a. Thank God—work of God in their lives.
   b. Love—*agape,* unmerited love.
   c. Faith—faith of God.
   d. Lord Jesus Christ and all saints—includes all.
   e. Communication—sharing.
   f. Effectual—powerful influence upon, effective.

B. What does the passage mean? (Interpretation)
1. What is the paragraph context?
   Paul is thanking God for His work in the lives of
   the Colossian Christians, and praying that their
   witness of love and faith will have a powerful
   influence and impact on the community.

2. What is the chapter context?
   This follows his greeting and precedes his appeal
   to Philemon on behalf of Onesimus.

3. What is the book context?
   Paul expects Philemon and the Colossian Christians to follow his advice so that their witness would be effective in the community and that he also would be able to thank God and rejoice when he comes to see them.

4. What is the testament context?
   Paul often thanks God in his letters for the work God has done in the lives of converts.

5. What is the Bible context?
   Real love and faith come from God and bless all who are touched by these attributes. Faith without works of lovingkindness is dead.

6. What would the reader understand the point to be?
   That God's love and faith should be shown to all the saints without respecting social customs such as slavery. When others see this, it will have a powerful effect on them and bring many to Christ.

7. What would we understand the point to be?
   That God's love and faith should be shown to all the saints without respecting persons. When others see this, it will have a powerful effect and bring many to Christ.

C. What does the passage mean to me? (Application)
1. A principle or truth to learn?
   God's love is no respecter of persons. It transcends all barriers, cultures, customs, etc.

2. An attitude to adopt?
   We should not be respecters of persons, but we should treat *all* Christians the same.

3. Paragraph (Appeal for Onesimus—verses 8-21)

A. What does the passage say? (Observation)

1. What is the main subject?

    Paul appeals to Philemon on behalf of Onesimus.

2. What are the main points?

    a. Onesimus is now a Christian.

    b. He was not useful, but now he will be.

    c. Paul could demand that Philemon take Onesimus back, but instead he asks, giving Philemon freedom of choice.

    d. Paul is a co-partner with Philemon. At the same time, he is Onesimus' friend.

    e. Paul asks Philemon to take Onesimus back, not as a runaway slave, but as a Christian brother. He even adopts him into the family as a son.

    f. Paul will take the responsibility for Onesimus' debts.

3. What are the main phrases?

    a. Receive him willingly.

    b. Receive him as a brother.

    c. Receive him as myself.

    d. Put his debt to my account.

    e. I will repay it.

4. What are the main words?

    a. Receive.

    b. Servant.

    c. Brother.

    d. Partner.

    e. Repay.

5. What do the main words mean?

    a. Receive—welcome and accept in full.

    b. Servant—slave.

c. Brother—kinsman.
d. Partner—having something in common.
e. Repay—to pay a penalty or fine.

B. What does the passage mean? (Interpretation)
1. What is the paragraph context?
   Paul is appealing to Philemon to take Onesimus back, to treat him as a Christian brother, to adopt him into his family, and to charge Paul for any of Onesimus' debts. Paul could demand this, but instead he gives Philemon the opportunity to respond willingly out of love.

2. What is the chapter context?
   Onesimus has now become a Christian and will be useful to Philemon.

3. What is the book context?
   This paragraph is the main point of the book.

4. What is the testament context?
   Onesimus will return to Philemon and be accompanied by Tychicus. (See Col. 4:7-9.)

5. What is the Bible context?
   Christ transforms all earthly relationships.

6. What would the reader understand the point to be?
   Paul was asking Philemon to receive Onesimus back as a Christian brother and adopt him into his own family. Paul promises to pay any debts Onesimus may owe to Philemon.

7. What would we understand the point to be?
   We should receive each other and forgive each other when there is repentance regardless of who the person is or what he has done.

137

C. What does the passage mean to me? (Application)
1. Attitude to adopt—to receive one another in the Lord.
2. Truth to learn—God took the handwriting of ordinances that was against us (our Certificate of Debt), and nailed it to the cross of Jesus. Because Jesus has interceded for us, we are no longer slaves to sin and the devil, on the run from God, but have become His children by faith in Christ Jesus. (See Col. 2:13-14.)

4. **Paragraph** (Closing—verses 22-25)
   A. What does the passage say? (Observation)
   1. What is the main subject?
      This contains Paul's closing comments.

   2. What are the main points?
      Paul asks Philemon to prepare a room for him because he hopes God will allow him to go to Colosse to see Philemon. He also makes note of Philemon's prayer and sends greetings from the others who are with him in Rome.

   3. What are the main phrases?
      Prepare me a lodging.
      Thank you for your prayers.
      I shall be given unto you.
      There salute thee.

   4. What are the main words?
      a. Fellowprisoners.
      b. Fellowlabourers.

   5. What do the main words mean?
      a. Fellowprisoners—sharing in the bondage.
      b. Fellowlabourers—sharing in the work.

B. What does the passage mean? (Interpretation)
1. What is the paragraph context?
   This is Paul's closing to his letter. It is similar to his closing remarks in his other letters.

2. What is the chapter context?
   (Same as above.)

3. What is the book context?
   (Same as above.)

4. What is the testament context?
   (Same as above.)

5. What is the Bible context?
   (Same as above.)

6. What would the reader understand the point to be?
   (Same as above.)

7. What would we understand the point to be?
   (Same as above.)

C. What does the passage mean to me? (Application)
1. Pray for one another.
2. Maintain fellowship.
3. Include everybody.

PHASE 3—BOOK SUMMARY

1. Purpose and Theme

A. What is the main purpose of the book?
Philemon was a slave owner in Colosse. One of his slaves, Onesimus, ran away and found Paul in jail in Rome. He was converted through Paul's witness. Paul wrote his friend Philemon to take Onesimus back. He asks Philemon to receive Onesimus, not as a slave, but as a Christian brother and to adopt Onesimus into his own family as a son. Paul also takes the responsibility for any of Onesimus' debts to Philemon.

B. What is the main theme of the book?
The book pictures Jesus Christ as the co-partner with God who became our friend in order to reconcile us to God so that we no longer have to be slaves to sin and the devil, on the run from God, but may become the children of God by faith in Jesus Christ. God has made this possible by putting our sins to the account of Jesus and putting His righteousness to our account. In this way, mercy and justice have been served without compromising either.

Philemon represents God, the Father.

Paul represents Jesus Christ.

Onesimus represents the human race.

2. Final Outline

A. What is the final outline of the book?

1. Greeting (verses 1-3).
   a. From Paul and Timothy.
   b. To Philemon, his family and church that meets in his house.
   c. Grace and peace extended to them.

2. Thanksgiving (verses 4-7).
   a. Thanks to God.
   b. Love and faith.
   c. Towards all saints.
   d. Powerful witness.

3. Paul's appeal for Onesimus (verses 8-21).
   a. Onesimus has now become a Christian.
   b. Paul asks rather than demands.
   c. Paul is co-partner with Philemon while, at the same time, the friend to Onesimus.
   d. Paul asks Philemon to take Onesimus back.
   e. Paul will take responsibility for Onesimus' debts.

4. Closing (verses 22-25).
   a. Paul plans to go to Colosse.
   b. Philemon is praying for Paul.
   c. All send their greeting.

3. Main Subjects

A. What are the main subjects in each chapter?
   1. Greeting.
   2. Thanksgiving.
   3. Paul's appeal.
   4. Closing.

B. What main point is made in each subject?
   1. Greeting—lovingly greet everyone affected by the problem.

2. Thanksgiving—The love and faith of God should flow out of us towards all believers as a witness and comfort to those around us.
3. Paul's appeal—God has reconciled us to himself through Jesus Christ who became our sin substitute on the cross.
4. Closing—we need each other.

4. Final Application

A. How can I apply each point to my life?
   1. I should greet my Christian brothers and sisters in the love of Jesus Christ.
   2. The love and faith of God should flow out of me.
   3. I should be an intercessor and mediator for others as Paul was for Onesimus, and I should encourage others to live uprightly.
   4. I should pray for others and fellowship with my brothers and sisters.

B. What false teaching does the book expose?
   Any system that destroys the worth and dignity of human life is wrong.

Review Exercise 9

1. List the three phases of a book study. Briefly mention the purpose of each phase.

    a.

    b.

    c.

2. List the three basic questions to answer for a subject paragraph within a chapter.

    a.

    b.

    c.

11

How to Study a Topic in the Bible

Have you ever wondered what the Bible says about a particular topic or subject? Of course, we all have. But how can we know? How can we find out? Where do we begin? How do we pull it all together? Part of the solution is knowing how to research a topic in the Bible effectively. And as I mentioned in the last chapter, knowing what questions to ask is important too. So, in this lesson we are going to discover how to study and research a topic in the Bible.

How to Do a Topical Study

There are *five basic steps* to take in studying a topic in the Bible. These are: 1. Select the appropriate topic. 2. Look up references to the topic. 3. Arrange key verses by main points. 4. Choose examples that illustrate the main points. 5. Develop a topical outline.

Bible Topic Analysis Form

There is a Bible Topic Analysis Form at the end of this chapter that will help you. You will need to refer to it as we go through these five steps. You could also copy this form in your study notebook, leaving the appropriate space between the questions for recording your answers. There is also a completed sample topical analysis using the sovereignty of God as an example.

Step 1—Select an Appropriate Topic.

The first step is to decide what topic you are going to study. There are various considerations that can guide you and help you narrow down your choice. For example, you may have a problem in your life which needs to be corrected. Or maybe it is a problem with someone close to you. Perhaps someone has asked you about something in the Bible and you could not answer the question. Current events may also trigger a need to study a particular topic. Maybe it is a topic that is being discussed and you realize you don't understand it. Or perhaps it is a topic you have never really studied for yourself. It could be a topic that you have studied, but for which you need further enlightenment. These types of considerations can help you select a topic that is relevant to your needs and the needs of those around you.

Step 2—Look Up Topic References.

After you select the appropriate topic, you must look up the Bible references to the topic. *The best way to do this is to use a Bible concordance.* A Bible concordance contains all the verses in the Bible on any given topic. We'll talk more about the Bible concordance in chapter twelve. Look up every relevant verse you can find in the Bible concordance that pertains to your subject. Then write down these Scripture references in the appropriate places in your study notebook.

Once you have listed all the Scripture references, look them up in your Bible. Normally, there will be many more Scripture references than you will need. So, try to determine which Scriptures are the key verses. Use these key verses for the rest of your study. Some of the key verses may be repetitious; that is, they may say the same thing using different words. *Group the repetitive key verses together.* Then determine which of the key verses are the most clear. Choose two or three from each group. These will be your main verses for the rest of your study. Keep the other key verses which you did not choose as references.

Step 3—Arrange Key Verses by Main Points.

You now want to determine what main point is made by the key verses. Study each one carefully. Then note which key verses make the same point. Group them together if you have not already done so. *Then arrange the main points into an order.*

Step 4—Choose Examples That Illustrate Main Points.

One of the best ways to learn is through examples. Jesus often taught by giving examples. And of course His life was the greatest teaching example. *So, you want to find examples from the Bible to illustrate each main point.*

First of all, try to find an Old Testament example. The things that happened to people in the Old Testament are examples from which we can learn. (See 1 Cor. 10:6; James 5:10.) Then see what Jesus said about the subject or how His life illustrated the point. Look for other New Testament examples as well. Determine how you can apply the example to your own life and share it with others.

Step 5—Develop a Topical Outline.

Finally, develop an outline of what you have learned. The outline would begin with an introduction explaining the topic followed by a statement of each point with Scripture references and illustrations and a concluding statement concerning the application of the topic to our lives.

Bible Doctrines

One of the most important topics to study is the subject of

Bible doctrines. *Bible doctrines are those teachings from the Bible that are unique to Christianity.* Taken together they represent the basic foundation of the Christian faith. *Since our actions are based on what we believe, it is very important that every Christian have a good knowledge of the basic Bible doctrines.* Basic Bible doctrines include such topics as: The authority of the Bible; the nature of God; the person and work of Christ; the Holy Spirit; the nature of man; the walk with God; the nature of the Church; the end times and future events.

Study Outlines

In the rest of this chapter, you will find eight "mini-outlines" that cover the basic Bible doctrines. It will help you to study each one in the order given and take the time to look up the Scripture references. There are many more Scriptures other than the ones given, but these will help you get started in the right direction. You can add others as you discover them in your own personal study.

STUDY OUTLINE NUMBER 1
A. *Knowing the Bible*
   1. The Authority of the Bible.
      (2 Tim. 3:16)
   2. The Purpose of the Bible.
      (2 Tim. 3:16-17)
   3. Commandment to Study the Bible.
      (Deut. 6:6-7; Josh. 1:8; 2 Tim. 2:15)
   4. Story of the Bible.
      (Luke 24:25-27, 44-47)
   5. Teacher of the Bible.
      (John 14:26, 16:13)

STUDY OUTLINE NUMBER 2
B. *Knowing God*
   1. God's Witness to His Existence.
      (Ps. 19:1; Rom. 1:18-19; 2 Tim. 3:16; John 14:8-9)

2. God's Personality.
    A. Self-Existing (Exod. 3:13-14).
    B. Spirit (John 4:24).
    C. Personal (Prov. 9:10).
    D. Unity (Deut. 6:4).
    E. Trinity (Matt. 28:19).
3. God's Majestic Attributes.
    A. Sovereign (Ps. 47:6-8).
    B. All Power (Rev. 19:6).
    C. All Knowledge (1 John 3:20).
    D. Everywhere Present (Jer. 23:23-24).
    E. Never Changing (Mal. 3:6).
4. God's Moral Attributes.
    A. Holy (Rev. 15:4).
    B. Loving (1 John 4:7-8).
    C. Just (Deut. 32:4).
    D. Good (Ps. 34:8).

STUDY OUTLINE NUMBER 3
C. *Knowing Jesus Christ*
    1. His Deity.
       (Isa. 9:6; Mic. 5:2; John 1:1; John 20:28)
    2. His Humanity.
       (John 1:14; Gal. 4:4-6; Heb. 2:14-18)
    3. His Substitutionary Death.
       (Rom. 3:20-25, 6:23, 10:9-10; 2 Cor. 5:21)
    4. His Resurrection.
       (Matt. 16:21, 28:1-6; John 20:11-17)
    5. His Exaltation.
       (Acts 1:9-11, 2:30; Eph. 1:20-23; Rev. 1:10-18)
    6. His Return.
       (John 14:1-3; 1 Thess. 4:13-17; Rev. 19:11-16)

STUDY OUTLINE NUMBER 4
D. *Knowing the Holy Spirit*
    1. His Personality.
       (John 14:16-17, 26, 16:7-15)

2. His Work in Regeneration.
   (John 3:1-7; Titus 3:5)
3. His Indwelling.
   (John 4:13-14, 7:37-39, 14:17)
4. His Sealing.
   (Eph. 1:13, 4:30)
5. His Filling.
   (Eph. 5:18; Acts 1:8, 2:4, 4:8, 31)

STUDY OUTLINE NUMBER 5
E. *Knowing Man*
   1. Created in God's Image.
      (Gen. 1:26-27; 1 Thess. 5:23-24)
   2. Man's Original Sin.
      (Gen. 2:15-17, 3:1-24)
   3. Sin Nature Inherited.
      (Rom. 5:12, 19; Mark 7:14-23; Jer. 17:9)
   4. Sin Separates Man From God.
      (Rom. 3:10-12; John 3:16-20; Isa. 59:1-2)
   5. Natural Man Cannot Know God.
      (1 Cor. 2:9-14)
   6. Man Cannot Earn His Way Back to God.
      (Isa. 64:6; Eph. 2:8-9; Titus 3:5-7)
   7. Man Reconciled to God.
      (Rom. 8:1, 14-17; Gal. 4:4-7)

STUDY OUTLINE NUMBER 6
F. *Living the Abundant Christian Life*
   1. Knowing Your Dominion.
      (Rom. 6:14, 8:11; 1 John 4:4)
   2. Identifying With Christ.
      (Rom. 6:3-14; Gal. 2:20)
   3. Appropriating His Lordship.
      (Rom. 12:1-2; John 12:24-26)
   4. Walking in the Spirit.
      (Eph. 5:18; Gal. 5:16-25)
   5. Wearing the Armor.
      (Eph. 6:10-18)

STUDY OUTLINE NUMBER 7

G. *The Nature of the Church*
1. What Is the Church?
    (Matt. 16:13-18)
2. The Purpose of the Church.
    (Acts 15:14; Eph. 3:10, 21)
3. The Nature of the Church.
    A. The Body of Christ.
        (1 Cor. 12:12-27; Eph. 1:22-23; Col. 1:18)
    B. The Bride of Christ.
        (2 Cor. 11:2; Eph. 5:23-32; Rev. 21:7-9)
    C. The Temple of God.
        (Eph. 2:20-22; 1 Cor. 3:16, 6:16, 19-20)
    D. The Priesthood of God.
        (1 Pet. 2:5-9; Rev. 5:9-10, 20:6)
    E. The Flock of God.
        (John 10:1-16, 27-28, 21:15-17; Acts 20:28)
    F. The Branches.
        (John 15:1-16; Gal. 5:22-25)

STUDY OUTLINE NUMBER 8

H. *End Times and Future Events*
1. Signs of His Coming.
    (Matt. 24; 2 Pet. 3:3-6; 2 Tim. 3:1-5, 4:1-4)
2. Judgment of Christians.
    (Rom. 14:10-12; 1 Cor. 3:9-15, 9:27, 4:5; 2 Cor. 5:10)
3. Seven-Year Tribulation.
    (Deut. 4:30; Dan. 12:1; Matt. 24; Rev. 6-18)
4. Second Coming of Christ.
    (Rev. 19:11-16)
5. The Millennium.
    (Rev. 20:1-10)
6. Great White Throne Judgment.
    (Rev. 20:11-15)
7. New Heaven and New Earth.
    (Rev. 21-22)

Sample Topical Analysis

The sample topical analysis which follows is based on the sovereignty of God. Many people are confused about this topic. Therefore, it is important that we have some understanding of the subject. Since the topic is already determined, the example begins with Step 2. All Scripture quotations in the example are from the King James Version. You may want to use this example to gain practice and experience in studying Bible topics. If you start with the Scripture references which are provided, you can then complete the Bible Topic Analysis Form for the rest of the study. If you are in a Bible study group, you may want to do this together. Share your results with the other members and then look over the example. The Scripture references are followed by blank forms for your personal notes and the completed example.

BIBLE TOPIC ANALYSIS FORM

STEP 1—Select an Appropriate Topic

A. What need do I have in my own life?
B. What need do those around me have?
C. What topic have I been asked about and couldn't answer?
D. What topic is currently being discussed?
E. What topic do I not fully understand?
F. What topic have I never studied for myself?

STEP 2—Look Up Topic References

A. Where are the topic Scripture references?
B. Which Scriptures are the key verses?
C. Which key verses are repetitive? (Group them.)
D. Which key verses are most clear?

STEP 3—Arrange Key Verses by Main Points

A. What point does the key verse make?
B. What other key verses make the same point?
C. Which are the main points? (Arrange them.)

STEP 4—Choose Examples That Illustrate Main Points

A. What is an Old Testament example?
B. How did Jesus illustrate the point?
C. What are other New Testament examples?
D. How do I apply the point to my life?

STEP 5—Develop a Topical Outline

A. What is an outline for the topic lesson?

SAMPLE TOPICAL ANALYSIS
Step 2: Look Up Topic References

A. Scripture References (Partial List)

Psalms 47:6-8, "Sing praises to God, sing praises: sing praises unto our King, sing praises. For God is the King of all the earth: sing ye praises with understanding. God reigneth over the heathen."

Psalms 24:1, "The earth is the Lord's, and the fulness thereof; the world, and they that dwell therein."

Daniel 4:17, "The most High ruleth in the kingdom of men, and giveth it to whomsoever he will, and setteth up over it the basest of men."

Job 38:4, "Where wast thou when I laid the foundations of the earth?"

Daniel 4:25, "The most High ruleth in the kingdom of men, and giveth it to whomsoever he will."

Psalms 83:18, "That men may know that thou, whose name alone is Jehovah, art the most high over all the earth."

Psalms 115:3, "But our God is in the heavens: he hath done whatsoever he hath pleased."

Psalms 135:6-7, "Whatsoever the Lord pleased, that did he in heaven, and in earth, in the seas, and all deep places. He causeth the vapours to ascend from the ends of the earth; he maketh lightnings from the rain; he bringeth the wind out of his treasuries."

Daniel 4:32, "The most High ruleth in the kingdom of men, and giveth it to whomsoever he will."

Genesis 1:3, "And God said, Let there be light: and there was light."

Jeremiah 10:12-13, "He hath made the earth by his power, he hath established the world by his wisdom, and hath stretched out the heavens by his discretion. When he uttereth his voice, there is a multitude of waters in the heavens, and he causeth the vapours to ascend from the ends of the earth; he maketh lightnings with rain, and bringeth forth the wind out of his treasuries."

Psalms 22:28, "For the kingdom is the Lord's: and he is the governor among the nations."

Daniel 4:35, "He doeth according to his will in the army of heaven, and among the inhabitants of the earth: and none can stay his hand."

1 Chronicles 29:11-12, "Thine, O Lord, is the greatness, and the power, and the glory, and the victory, and the majesty: for all that is in the heaven and in the earth is thine; thine is the kingdom, O Lord, and thou art exalted as head above all. Both riches and honour come of thee, and thou reignest over all; and in thine hand is power and might; and in thine hand it is to make great, and to give strength unto all."

Psalms 33:6-9, "By the word of the Lord were the heavens made; . . . He gathereth the waters of the sea together as an heap: he layeth up the depth in storehouses. . . . For he spake, and it was done; he commanded, and it stood fast."

Job 26:7, "He stretcheth out the north over the empty place, and hangeth the earth upon nothing."

Proverbs 16:9, "A man's heart deviseth his way: but the Lord directeth his steps."

Proverbs 21:30, "There is no wisdom nor understanding nor counsel against the Lord."

Mark 4:41, "What manner of man is this, that even the wind and the sea obey him?"

Proverbs 19:21, "There are many devices in a man's heart; nevertheless the counsel of the Lord, that shall stand."

John 19:11, "Thou couldest have no power at all against me, except it were given thee from above . . . ."

James 4:15, "If the Lord will, we shall live, and this do, or that."

Genesis 45:7-8, "And God sent me before you to preserve you a posterity in the earth, and to save your lives by a great deliverance. So now it was not you that sent me hither, but God . . . ."

Revelation 17:17, "For God hath put it in their hearts to fulfil his will, and to agree, and give their kingdom unto the beast, until the words of God shall be fulfilled."

Acts 17:28, "For in him we live, and move, and have our being . . . ."

B. Key Verses

Step 2: Look Up Topic References

B. Key Verses (Continued)

158

Step 2: Look Up Topic References

C. Key Verses Grouped

C. Key Verses Grouped (Continued)

Step 2: Look Up Topic References

D. Clearest Key Verses

Similar Points Made by Key Verses
(Questions A-C)

Step 3: Arrange Key Verses by Main Points

Similar Points Made by Key Verses (Continued)
(Questions A-C)

Step 4: Choose Examples That Illustrate Main Point

Step 5: Lesson Outline

B. Key Verses

Psalms 47:6-8, "Sing praises to God, sing praises: sing praises unto our King, sing praises. For God is the King of all the earth: sing ye praises with understanding. God reigneth over the heathen."

Psalms 24:1, "The earth is the Lord's, and the fulness thereof; the world, and they that dwell therein."

Daniel 4:17, "The most High ruleth in the kingdom of men, and giveth it to whomsoever he will, and setteth up over it the basest of men."

Daniel 4:25, "The most High ruleth in the kingdom of men, and giveth it to whomsoever he will."

Psalms 115:3, "But our God is in the heavens: he hath done whatsoever he hath pleased."

Psalms 135:6-7, "Whatsoever the Lord pleased, that did he in heaven, and in earth, in the seas, and all deep places. He causeth the vapours to ascend from the ends of the earth; he maketh lightnings from the rain; he bringeth the wind out of his treasuries."

Daniel 4:32, "The most High ruleth in the kingdom of men, and giveth it to whomsoever he will."

Genesis 1:3, "And God said, Let there be light: and there was light."

Jeremiah 10:12-13, "He hath made the earth by his power, he hath established the world by his wisdom, and hath stretched out the heavens by his discretion. When he uttereth his voice, there is a multitude of waters in the heavens, and he causeth the vapours to ascend from the ends of the earth; and maketh lightnings with rain, and bringeth forth the wind out of his treasuries."

B. Key Verses (Continued)

Psalms 22:28, "For the kingdom is the Lord's: and he is the governor among the nations."

Daniel 4:35, "He doeth according to his will in the army of heaven, and among the inhabitants of the earth: and none can stay his hand."

1 Chronicles 29:11-12, "Thine, O Lord, is the greatness and the power, and the glory, and the victory, and the majesty: for all that is in the heaven and in the earth is thine; thine is the kingdom, O Lord, and thou art exalted as head above all. Both riches and honour come of thee, and thou reignest over all; and in thine hand it is to make great, and to give strength unto all."

Psalms 33:6-9, "By the word of the Lord were the heavens made: . . . He gathereth the waters of the sea together as an heap: he layeth up the depth in storehouses. . . . For he spake, and it was done; he commanded, and it stood fast."

Proverbs 16:9, "A man's heart deviseth his way: but the Lord directeth his steps."

Proverbs 21:30, "There is no wisdom, nor understanding nor counsel against the Lord."

Mark 4:41, "What manner of man is this, that even the wind and the sea obey him?"

Proverbs 19:21, "There are many devices in a man's heart; nevertheless the counsel of the Lord, that shall stand."

John 19:11, "Thou couldest have no power at all against me, except it were given thee from above. . . ."

James 4:15, "If the Lord will, we shall live, and this do, or that."

C. Key Verses Grouped

Group 1

Psalms 47:6-8, "Sing praises to God, sing praises: sing praises unto our King, sing praises. For God is the King of all the earth: sing ye praises with understanding. God reigneth over the heathen."

Psalms 24:1, "The earth is the Lord's, and the fulness thereof; the world, and they that dwell therein."

Psalms 115:3, "But our God is in the heavens: he hath done whatsoever he hath pleased."

1 Chronicles 29:11-12, "Thine, O Lord, is the greatness, and the power, and the glory, and the victory, and the majesty: for all that is in the heaven and in the earth is thine; thine is the kingdom, O Lord, and thou art exalted as head above all. Both riches and honour come of thee, and thou reignest over all; and in thine hand it is to make great, and to give strength unto all."

Group 2

Daniel 4:17, "The most High ruleth in the kingdom of men, and giveth it to whomsoever he will, and setteth up over it the basest of men."

Daniel 4:25, "The most High ruleth in the kingdom of men, and giveth it to whomsoever he will."

Daniel 4:32, ". . . the most High ruleth in the kingdom of men, and giveth it to whomsoever he will."

Daniel 4:35, ". . . he doeth according to his will in the army of heaven, and among the inhabitants of the earth: and none can stay his hand."

C. Key Verses Grouped (Continued)

Psalms 22:28, "For the kingdom is the Lord's: and he is the governor among the nations."

John 19:11, "Thou couldest have no power at all against me, except it were given thee from above . . . ."

Group 3

Psalms 135:6-7, "Whatsoever the Lord pleased, that did he in heaven, and in earth, in the seas, and all deep places. He causeth the vapours to ascend from the ends of the earth; he maketh lightnings from the rain; he bringeth the wind out of his treasuries."

Jeremiah 10:12-13, "He hath made the earth by his power, he hath established the world by his wisdom, and hath stretched out the heavens by his discretion. When he uttereth his voice, there is a multitude of waters in the heavens, and he causeth the vapours to ascend from the ends of the earth; and maketh lightnings with rain, and bringeth forth the wind out of his treasuries."

Genesis 1:3, "And God said, Let there be light: and there was light."

Psalms 33:6-9, "By the word of the Lord were the heavens made; . . . He gathereth the waters of the sea together as an heap: he layeth up the depth in storehouses. . . . For he spake, and it was done; he commanded, and it stood fast."

Mark 4:41, "What manner of man is this, that even the wind and the sea obey him?"

169

C. Key Veres Grouped (Continued)

Group 4

Proverbs 16:9, "A man's heart deviseth his way: but the Lord directeth his steps."

Proverbs 21:30, "There is no wisdom nor understanding nor counsel against the Lord."

Proverbs 19:21, "There are many devices in a man's heart; nevertheless the counsel of the Lord, that shall stand."

James 4:15, "If the Lord will, we shall live, and this do, or that."

D. Clearest Key Verses

Group 1

Psalms 47:6-8, "Sing praises to God, sing praises: sing praises unto our King, sing praises. For God is the King of all the earth: sing ye praises with understanding. God reigneth over the heathen."

1 Chronicles 29:11-12, "Thine, O Lord, is the greatness, and the power, and the glory, and the victory, and the majesty: for all that is in the heaven and in the earth is thine; thine is the kingdom, O Lord, and thou art exalted as head above all. Both riches and honour come of thee, and thou reignest over all; all in thine hand it is to make great, and to give strength unto all."

Group 2

Daniel 4:25, "The most High ruleth in the kingdom of men, and giveth it to whomsoever he will."

Psalms 22:28, "For the kingdom is the Lord's: and he is the governor among the nations."

John 19:11, "Thou couldest have no power at all against me, except it were given thee from above . . . ."

Group 3

Psalms 135:6-7, "Whatsoever the Lord pleased, that did he in heaven, and in earth, in the seas, and all deep places. He causeth the vapours to ascend from the ends of the earth; he maketh lightnings from the rain; he bringeth the wind out of his treasuries."

D. Clearest Key Verses (Continued)

Mark 4:41, "What manner of man is this, that even the wind and the sea obey him?"

Group 4

Proverbs 16:9, "A man's heart deviseth his way: but the Lord directeth his steps."

Proverbs 21:30, "There is no wisdom nor understanding nor counsel against the Lord."

Proverbs 19:21, "There are many devices in a man's heart; nevertheless the counsel of the Lord, that shall stand."

James 4:15, "If the Lord will, we shall live, and this do, or that."

Similar Points Made by Key Verses
(Questions A-C)

Group 1

A. God Is Sovereign

Psalms 47:6-8, "Sing praises to God, sing praises: sing praises unto our King, sing praises. For God is the *King of all the earth:* sing praises with understanding. *God reigneth over the heathen . . . .*"

1 Chronicles 29:11-12, "Thine, O Lord, is the greatness, and the power, and the glory, and the victory, and the majesty: for *all that is in the heaven and in the earth is thine;* thine is the kingdom O Lord, and thou art exalted as *head above all. . . .* and in thine hand is power and might; and in thine hand it is to make great, and to give strength unto all.*"

Group 2

B. God Is Sovereign Over the Nations

Daniel 4:25, "The most High *ruleth in the kingdom of men,* and *giveth it to whomsoever he will."*

Psalms 22:28, "For the kingdom is the Lord's: and he is the *governor among the nations."*

John 19:11, "Thou couldest have no power at all against me, except it were *given thee from above . . . ."*

Group 3

C. God Is Sovereign Over Nature

Psalms 135:6-7, "*Whatsoever the Lord pleased,* that did he in *heaven,* and in *earth,* in the *seas,* and *all* deep places. *He* causeth the vapours to ascend from the ends of the earth; *he* maketh lightnings from the rain; *he* bringeth the wind out of *his* treasuries."

Mark 4:41, "What manner of man is this, that even *the wind and the sea obey him?*"

Group 4

D.   *God Is Sovereign Over Individuals*

Proverbs 16:9, "A man's heart deviseth his way: but *the Lord directeth his steps.*"

Proverbs 21:30, "There is no wisdom nor understanding nor counsel *against the Lord.*"

Proverbs 19:21, "There are many devices in a man's heart; *nevertheless the counsel of the Lord, that shall stand.*"

James 4:15, "*If the Lord will,* we shall live, and this do, or that."

Step 4: Choose Examples That Illustrate the Main Point

1. *God Is Sovereign.*
   A. Define.
   B. Give Scripture References.

2. *God Is Sovereign Over the Nations.*
   A. Old Testament Example—Dream by Nebuchadnezzar (Dan. 2:31-45).
   B. How Jesus Illustrated—Rome couldn't take Him unless God allowed it (John 19:11).
   C. Other New Testament Examples—Nations give allegiance to the beast (Rev. 17:17).
   D. Personal Application—Rest and peace knowing God is totally in charge and everything is right on schedule

3. *God Is Sovereign Over Nature*
   A. Old Testament Example—Old Testament Miracles (Red Sea).
   B. How Jesus Illustrated—Walking on the water.
   C. Other New Testament Examples—Seals in Revelation.
   D. Personal Application—Peace in midst of bad weather, prayer for protection against elements, prayer for use of elements for glory of God.

4. *God Is Sovereign Over Individuals*
   A. Old Testament Example—Joseph (Gen. 45:7-8, 50:20).
   B. How Jesus Illustrated—Jews couldn't take Him until His time was ready.
   C. Other New Testament Examples—beast and false prophet cast into hell (Rev. 19:20).
   D. Personal Application—Recognize God's claim on our lives and submit our wills to His.

Step 5: Lesson Outline

---

1. *God Is Sovereign.*
   A. Sovereign—God is King of kings and Lord of lords and He is actively exercising absolute rule over all His creation.
   B. Scriptures (Ps. 47:6-8; 1 Chron. 29:11-12).

2. *God Is Sovereign Over the Nations* (Dan. 4:25; Ps. 22:28; John 19:11).
   A. Old Testament Example—Dream by Nebuchadnezzar (Dan. 2:31-45).
   B. How Jesus Illustrated—Rome couldn't take Him unless God allowed it (John 19:11).
   C. Other New Testament Examples—Nations give allegiance to the beast (Rev. 17:17).
   D. Personal Application—Rest and peace, knowing God is totally in charge and everything is right on schedule.

3. *God Is Sovereign Over Nature* (Ps. 135:6-7; Mark 4:41).
   A. Old Testament Example—Old Testament miracles (Red Sea).
   B. How Jesus Illustrated—Walking on the water (John 6:19).
   C. Other New Testament Examples—Seals in Revelation 6-18.
   D. Personal Application—Peace in midst of bad weather, prayer for protection against elements, prayer for use of elements for glory of God.

4. *God Is Sovereign Over Individuals* (Prov. 16:9, 19:21, 21:30; James 4:15).
   A. Old Testament Example—Joseph (Gen. 45:7-8, 50:20).
   B. How Jesus Illustrated—Jews couldn't take Him until His time was ready (John 8:20).
   C. Other New Testament Examples—beast and false prophet cast into hell.
   D. Personal Application—Recognize God's claim on our lives and submit our wills to His.

Review Exercise 10

1. List the five steps involved in studying a topic in the Bible.
   a.
   b.
   c.
   d.
   e.

2. Explain what we mean by the words "Bible doctrines."

3. State why it is important to understand Bible doctrines.

12

How to Understand the Bible

When we begin to read and study the Bible, we soon find that we don't understand what a lot of it means. Many verses are not clear to us. Other verses seem to be contradictory, while others seem to have more than one meaning. This can all be very confusing.

So, we sometimes have difficulty understanding the Bible. One of the reasons for this is that the Bible was written in a setting and language different from our own. The Bible writers lived, thought and expressed themselves differently than we do today. *Therefore, there are historical, cultural and language differences separating Bible times and our times.* This makes it difficult for us to understand the exact meaning of certain passages in the Bible. For this reason, we must interpret these passages in order to understand them. As we study this subject, we will explore the problems and principles associated with biblical interpretation.

The Problem of Interpretation

Before God called me to teach the Bible, I worked with computers. There was a machine I sometimes used called "the interpreter." The interpreter was a very important machine, and it had only one function: to read computer cards that had punches—no writing—in them, and to print on the cards what the punches meant. This would enable people to read the cards. Now the machine didn't interpret the punches in just any way. It followed certain rules to make sure its interpretation was correct. And all of the machines followed the same rules, so you could rely on what was printed on the cards. And you didn't have to be a scholar in computer language in order to use the cards. It did help in certain complex situations. But for the most part, it certainly wasn't necessary.

Do you see the parallel here? The differences separating Bible times from our times are like the punched holes in the computer cards. They must be interpreted. Now the Holy Spirit is the interpreter. And He lives in all of us who have had a spiritual rebirth through Jesus Christ. *God has given us the Holy Spirit and a renewed mind so that we can understand the Bible.* But that doesn't mean that we can interpret the Bible in any way we desire. This is how people get into real trouble. What they *say* the Bible means and what it *really* means are often two different things.

Principles of Interpretation

Frequently you hear people say, "But that's your opinion or your interpretation of what the Bible means." Well, of course, it's your opinion or interpretation. That's not the question. The question is: "How did you arrive at your interpretation or opinion?" Just like the machine, *there are certain principles or rules we must follow in order to properly interpret the Bible.* Bible scholars call these principles of interpretation "hermeneutics." They get this word from a character in Greek mythology named Hermes who was supposed to interpret the messages from the gods to the people.

In this lesson we are going to discuss five basic principles that help guide us to understand the Bible properly. *As long as you follow these principles with a humble, teachable spirit, you can have confidence in the Holy Spirit's ability to interpret the Scriptures to you.* This means you don't have to be a scholar in the Hebrew and Greek languages in order to understand the Bible. It is very valuable and does help in certain complex situations. But, for the most part, it is certainly not necessary to know the original languages of the Bible in order to understand the Bible.

1. Interpret the Bible in Its Literal Sense.
A. Literal Statements.

We should always interpret the Bible in its literal sense unless the context clearly indicates otherwise. What do I mean by "literal sense"? The literal sense is the normal sense or natural meaning of words and sentence structures. It does not appear that God wrote the Bible in "Holy Ghost language." So, we take the language of the Bible as we do that of any other book—a noun is still a noun, and a verb is still a verb.

When you read a book, you seek to understand it according to the normal meaning of the words and word relationships in the structure of the sentences. You read the Bible in the same manner. For example, suppose you checked out a book from the library and in it you read a sentence, "And Judas went and hanged himself." What would you think the writer meant by that? In all probability, you would think he meant just what he said. There was a person in the story named Judas who, for some reason, went out and hanged himself. Now you put that book down and begin to read your Bible. You come to a sentence that tells you that Judas went and hanged himself. (See Matt. 27:5.) Now what do you think Matthew meant by that? Just what he said. There was a person in the Bible named Judas who went and hanged himself.

Suppose you read in the Bible, "Now the Lord had prepared a great fish to swallow up Jonah. And Jonah was in the belly of the fish three days and three nights" (See Jon. 1:17, KJV). What do you think that might mean? Well, I think it means just what it says.

Some people try to find a hidden meaning behind every word in the Bible. They spiritualize or allegorize much of what they read so that nothing means what it says. The result is that they have all kinds of weird interpretations of what they think the Scriptures mean. This can lead them into serious error and unwise decisions.

B. Figurative Statements.

There are certain types of statements in the Bible, however, which should not be interpreted literally. These are called "figurative statements." *A figurative statement is a statement that is used to communicate something other than its normal, literal meaning.* We use figurative statements to help us make a certain point. For example, after overeating, you might say, "My eyes were bigger than my stomach." Of course, you don't mean that literally. It's just a figurative way of saying that you ate more than you should have.

Types of Figurative Statements

Figurative statements are normally easy to identify. The five more common types found in the Bible are as follows:

1. Metaphor.

A metaphor compares two differing things in a direct manner. For example, Jesus said, "I am the door: by me if any man enter in, he shall be saved, and shall go in and out, and find pasture" (John 10:9, KJV). Now we clearly realize that Jesus did not think He was a literal door. He was a human being. But, in the same way that you enter a room through its door, you come to God through Jesus Christ.

2. Simile.

A simile is like a metaphor except that the comparison includes the words "like" or "as." Jesus said, "If you have faith as a mustard seed, you will say to this mountain, 'move from here to there,' and it will move; and nothing will be impossible for you" (Matt. 17:20, NKJ). Jesus obviously meant that we can do great things with just a little faith.

3. Hyperbole.

Hyperbole involves making a deliberate exaggeration with the intent of emphasizing a point. We read, "And why do you look at the speck that is in your brother's eye, but do not consider the plank that is in your own eye?" (Matt. 7:8, NKJ). Again, it is obvious that Jesus did not mean that a human eye could contain a great, big plank. But He used this exaggeration to point out that we should not try to get a little sin out of another person's life until we get bigger sins out of our own lives.

4. Personification.

Personification is a figure of speech that gives personal characteristics to a non-living thing, as though it were a person. For example, "Let the floods clap their hands: let the hills be joyful together" (Ps. 98:8, KJV). We know that floods do not have hands, and that hills cannot express joy. This is simply a way of saying that all of creation declares the glory of God.

5. Parables.

A parable is a story that is told for the purpose of illustrating a spiritual or moral truth. Jesus often taught using parables. A parable usually has only one basic point to convey. To interpret a parable, try to find the central point without making something special and spiritual of all the details. The details are only there to bring out the point.

These, then, are the more common figurative statements in the Bible. As you can see, they are rather easy to identify. Except for these types of expressions, we should always interpret the Bible in its literal sense.

2. Interpret Scripture With Scripture.

One of my favorite expressions is that the Bible is its own

commentary. Although God used many men to write the Bible, it tells only one story. And as we brought out in an earlier chapter, it tells this story with perfect unity and harmony. God has spread out His story through all sixty-six books in the Bible. Therefore, no portion of the Scriptures stands alone but is related to all the rest of the Bible.

Since God is the single author, He obviously is not going to say something in one part of the Bible and then contradict himself in another section. *There are no contradictions in the Bible.* If we think we have found a contradiction, we simply need to keep on reading and digging until we find the explanation for the apparent conflict. This means that anytime we interpret a passage of the Scriptures in such a way that our interpretation is in conflict with something else the Bible says, then our interpretation is wrong. *We just have to keep at it until our interpretation becomes consistent with the whole of the Scriptures.*

Let's consider the following example. Jesus said, "Judge not, that you be not judged" (Matt. 7:1, NKJ). When people read this statement, they think that they are never to say anything to another person about the way the individual is living. In their view, this would be judging, and Jesus said not to judge. But Paul says, "But he who is spiritual judges all things . . ."(1 Cor. 2:15, NKJ). Paul goes on to teach that we should judge those among us who claim to be Christians, but are living evil lives (See 1 Cor. 5:11-13).

Now there seems to be a conflict between the statements of Jesus and Paul. But on closer examination, we find that they are talking about different things. Jesus is talking about judging a person's motives, while Paul is talking about judging a person's actions. Unless God reveals them to us, we don't know a person's motives. We don't know why they do given things. We don't know what's in their hearts. And we should not judge them in this respect. But we are to judge people's actions by the Word of God. So, if a person claims to be a Christian, but lives in an evil way, we have a responsibility to deal with that situation according to the Scriptures. Otherwise, the Church could not function as light and salt.

Another example is in regard to works. Paul says we are saved by grace through faith alone and not by works. (See Eph. 2:8-10.) James, on the other hand, says that faith alone is not enough but that works are also necessary. (See James 2:24.) Again, we *seem* to have a conflict. But as with the preceding example, Paul and James are talking about different kinds of works. Paul is talking about works of self-righteousness. These are religious or moral works which a person does out of himself. Even though they may be good in man's eyes, they all flow out of a nature that is tainted by sin. Therefore, Paul says that they cannot save us. He confirms that this is what he means in Titus 3:5, where he says we are not saved by works of righteousness that we have done. James is talking about works of lovingkindness. These are works that flow out of a spirit that has been regenerated by the Holy Spirit. The Holy Spirit motivates us to perform the works that James speaks about out of the love of God. So, if a person has truly placed his faith in Jesus Christ, it will be evidenced by works of lovingkindness. This is the basis for James's statements. And Paul completely agrees with him when he talks about works of lovingkindness in other places in the Bible (See 1 Tim. 6:18; Titus 1:16, 2:14, 3:8). Here we see the perfect harmony of Scripture.

3. Interpret Scripture Within Its Context.

The context of a passage helps explain the meaning of the passage. For example, the meaning of a word can only be understood within the context of the sentence in which the word is located. A word is within the context of a sentence. A sentence is within the context of a paragraph. A paragraph is within the context of a chapter. A chapter is within the context of a book of the Bible. A book of the Bible is within the context of the Old or New Testaments. And the Old and New Testaments are within the context of the entire Bible.

Now we have all lifted verses out of context from time to time. And we can really get in big trouble when we do this. One verse that I often hear lifted out of context is

Philippians 4:19. It reads, "And my God shall supply all your need according to His riches in glory by Christ Jesus" (NKJ). Often we quote this verse to people to encourage them. But do you know the context of this verse? Paul was writing to the Christians at Philippi. These were very poor Christians. Yet they gave out of their poverty to support Paul. Initially, they were the only Christians who supported Paul. God will be no man's debtor. Therefore, Paul is able to say to them that God will supply all of their needs. But he didn't say that to the Colossians, or the Galatians, Ephesians, etc. He said that, in context, to the Philippians. Likewise, we need to understand Paul's remark in context. God has established principles of living and giving in the Bible. If we will abide by these principles, then God will supply all of our needs.

4. Interpret Scripture Historically.

The Bible was written by real people who lived in real places at real points in time. And they wrote out of their culture and background. *So, for us to properly interpret the Bible, we need some knowledge of the historical background from which the writers came.*

There are three basic types of information that we need to know about the historical background. First, it is important to get as much information as we can about the *historical setting* of the writing. For example, it helps to know that, in Paul's day, Philippi was a Roman colony. Therefore, when he wrote to the Philippian Christians that their citizenship was in heaven, we understand he was telling them that they were a colony of heaven on planet earth (See Phil. 3:20).

Knowledge of the *geographic setting* is also important. When Jesus was on planet earth, the land of Israel was divided into three areas which would be similar to our counties. The northern area was Galilee, the central area was Samaria and the southern area was Judea. For a Jew to travel from Judea to Galilee, or from Galilee to Judea, he had to pass through Samaria. But this is where the Samaritans lived. And the Jews hated the Samaritans because they were part Jew and part Gentile. So, the Jews would go far out of their way to keep from passing through Samaria. But this was not true of Jesus. He walked right through the hated Samaritan territory. This type of information gives us great insight into the conversation Jesus had with the Samaritan woman who met Him at Jacob's well (See John 4).

It is also helpful to have some knowledge about the *cultural setting*. For example, the book of Ruth tells us about a courtship custom. Ruth, the young widow, goes one night to the threshing floor where Boaz, her suitor, is sleeping. She uncovers his feet and lays down by them. When Boaz's feet get cold, he wakes up and realizes someone is there. When he asks who it is, Ruth reveals her identity and tells Boaz to spread his skirt over her for he is a near kinsman (see Ruth 3:9). Now this doesn't make any sense to us today. But if we understood the cultural setting, we would know that this was the normal way for a widow to ask a man to marry her. And, of course, this points us to Christ who became our near kinsman as a human and clothed us with His garment of salvation, making us His bride.

So, we do our best to reconstruct the actual historical situation in which God's Word was written. If we can understand God's Word to that situation we can better understand it to our own situations.

5. Interpret Scripture According to Correct Word Meanings.
The fifth principle is that we should interpret the *Scriptures according to the correct meanings of words.* Words are the basic building blocks of our communication. We have to understand words and word meanings in order know what people are talking about. *One of the problems in understanding words is that they change their meanings over a period of time.* About 400 words have changed meaning from the way they were used in the King James Bible. Some words change meaning in a short period of time.

Not too many years ago the word gay meant someone

who was happy. Today it refers to a homosexual. Today, the word prevent means to hinder. In King James's day it meant to precede. So, when Paul wrote about the Christian resurrection he said that we who are still alive will not prevent those who have already died (See 1 Thess. 4:15). We use the word conversation to refer to someone's speech. It used to refer to their manner of living. When Paul wrote the Christians about letting their conversation become the gospel, he was saying that we should live as Christians ought to live (See Phil. 1:27).

We need to understand the words in the Bible in order to understand the Bible properly. This means that when we study a passage, we need to look up the meaning of the key words and not just assume that we know what they mean. In our next chapter, we are going to see how to do this.

Review Exercise 11

1. Explain why it is necessary to interpret the Bible.

2. List the five principles of Bible interpretation.
   a.
   b.
   c.
   d.
   e.

3. Explain what figurative statements are.

4. List five types of figurative statements found in the Bible.
   a.
   b.
   c.
   d.
   e.

13
Basic Bible Study Aids

When I first began to study the Bible, I soon realized that the Bible did not take the time to explain the historical, geographic and cultural setting in which it was written. Nor did it explain the Hebrew and Greek languages and the meanings of words that were customarily used in Bible times. This certainly did not keep me from understanding the basic message of the Bible. But I knew I was missing a lot. So, I began to search for reference books that could provide me with helpful background information and word meanings. During my early search, I spent a lot of money buying books that I really did not need. I also spent a lot of unnecessary time reading them.

The Need for Study Aids
I think all new Bible students have this same problem. We learn the basic message of the Bible. But as we get deeper

into our study, we realize that we need some help to fill in the background details relating to the setting in which the Bible was written. People often ask me about study aids that can help them better understand the background setting of the Bible and the languages in which it was written. So, in this chapter, we are going to discuss some of these aids that can benefit you and that will help your Bible study become richer and more meaningful.

The Role of Study Aids

But before we begin, let's be reminded that *no book written by man can take the place of the Holy Spirit.* He is the teacher. And just having scholarly reference books is no guarantee that you will hear from God. The Bible is really the only book that is absolutely necessary.

However, the study aids we are going to discuss in this chapter certainly can and do help to enlarge our knowledge and appreciation of the Word of God.

Basic Bible Study Aids

1. A Bible for Reading and Studying.

I mention a Bible in this discussion because it is the best study aid for itself. Many people spend too much time reading books about the Bible. *But there is no substitute for reading and studying the Bible itself.* As we mentioned in an earlier chapter, it is helpful to read the Bible in a modern-language version. The most popular Bible for easy reading is the Living Bible. The Living Bible is published by Tyndale House Publishers. But remember that the feature of the Living Bible is that it is a paraphrase and not a direct, word-for-word translation. For this reason, it doesn't seem that the Living Bible would be appropriate as a study Bible, unless, of course, it is the only Bible available to you.

If you could only buy one study Bible, I believe the Open Bible edition of the King James Version would really benefit you. The Open Bible is packed with easy-to-use study aids. There is a brief introduction and outline before each book in the Bible. There is also what the publishers call a "Cyclopedic Index." This index provides reference pointers on 8,000 Bible subjects. There is also a helpful concordance. In addition, there are fourteen very good topical outlines on basic Bible doctrines. And there are many more study aids such as cross references and clarifications of words that have changed meaning over the years. The Open Bible is published by Thomas Nelson Publishers.

2. A Bible Study Notebook.

One of the reasons we fail to learn or we forget what we have already learned is because we don't write things down. *It is much easier for us to observe and remember things when we write them down.* An inexpensive spiral notebook is all that you need. Divide your notebook into two sections. Call one section Bible Books and the other section Bible Topics. Then copy the Bible Book Analysis Forms in one section and the Bible Topic Analysis Forms in the other section. This will give you a central place for writing down what God is teaching you. And it will be easy for you to find those things you have learned when you need to refer to them at a later date.

3. A Bible Concordance.

A Bible concordance gives a brief definition of the original Hebrew and Greek meanings of every word in the Bible. It also identifies the Hebrew or Greek word from which the English equivalent has been translated and lists every verse in the Bible where the words are used. *This, of course, is a great help in studying the meaning of words. It is also a great location finder.* Many times you may be able to remember only one or two words in a verse, but you can't remember where the verse is found. Well, you can find it easily with a concordance. You simply look up the word that you can remember in the concordance and you will find a listing of every verse in the Bible containing that word, with short quotes showing the contexts of the word. You can also use a concordance to find all the Bible references on any particular subject. This is very helpful when doing a topical study and saves you a lot of time in trying to find all the verses from scratch. The work has already been done for you. A widely used concordance is *Strong's Exhaustive Concordance*, published by Abingdon Press.

4. A Bible Dictionary.

A Bible dictionary is like a regular dictionary or an encyclopedia, except that it is about the Bible. *It contains complete alphabetic listings and brief descriptive explanations of every subject found in the Bible, along with Scripture references.* There are also many pictures that help the reader to visualize some of the topics which are being discussed. The Bible dictionary is one of the main sources where you can find information about the historical, geographic and cultural settings of the Bible. And you would make great use of it to get this helpful background. *The Pictorial Bible Dictionary* published by Zondervan Publishing House is helpful, as is the *International Bible Dictionary* published by Bridge Publishing, Inc..

5. A Bible Atlas.

A Bible atlas provides you with a collection of important maps that are relevant to Bible times. *These maps help to give you information about the geographic setting of the Bible.* With the help of an atlas you can actually take a survey of the Bible from a geographic perspective. One very helpful Bible atlas is *Atlas of the Bible Lands* published by Hammond, Incorporated.

6. A One-Volume Commentary.

It would also be helpful to have a one-volume commentary on the whole Bible. *This will give you a good survey of the entire Bible, consolidated into one book.* A commentary generally provides helpful introductory and background information on each book—such as its author, date, place and purpose. All of this will help you in your Book Analysis. You may want to consider the *Wycliffe Bible Commentary* published by Moody Press.

But when you read a commentary, remember that you are reading another person's opinion. The opinion of the commentator may not always be right. Therefore, you need to use a commentary primarily as a check and balance against your opinion from the Scriptures. Many times people will allow a commentary to form their opinion for them before they have studied the Scriptures for themselves. Then, when they do study, their opinion is prejudiced by what they have read in a commentary. *But always make your own investigation of the Bible first, then check your understanding against what others have said.* It is not necessary to agree with everything in the commentary in order to benefit from it.

A Final Word

We now come to the end of this book. But I hope it is just the beginning of your study of the Bible. As we have stated, God gave us the Bible so that we could know Him and walk with Him. He has written the Bible so that we can understand it. *And we can best understand it when we approach God with a humble spirit and a thinking mind renewed by the Holy Spirit, applying sound principles of interpretation.* When you do this, God will be faithful to speak His Word to you.

Chapter 13—Basic Bible Study Aids

Review Exercise 12

1. Explain the need for Bible study aids.

2. State the role of Bible study aids.

3. List the six basic Bible study aids. Briefly state the value of each.

   a.

   b.

   c.

   d.

   e.

   f.

BIBLE STUDY MATERIALS BY RICHARD BOOKER
MINISTRY IN THE LOCAL CHURCH

Richard currently spends most of his time in a traveling ministry to the local church. If you are interested in having him come to your church, contact him directly at his Houston address.

CHRISTIAN GROWTH SEMINARS

Richard conducts a series of unique seminars in the local church. Each seminar is six hours long with a workbook in which the participant writes during the seminar. Current seminars are on prayer, personal Bible study, successful Christian living, and discipleship. Brochures are available from the ministry.

LOCAL CHURCH CENTERED BIBLE SCHOOLS

Richard has developed a Christian Growth Institute, which is a nine-month Bible school designed to be taught in the local church by the pastor or his associates. A catalog is available from the ministry.

BOOKS

Richard's books are superior quality teaching books. They uniquely communicate profound life-changing Bible truths with a rich depth, freshness and simplicity, and also explain how to apply what you have read to your life. His books are described on the following pages. You may order them through your bookstore or clip and mail the Book Order Form provided in the back of this book.

THE MIRACLE OF THE SCARLET THREAD

This book explains how the Old and New Testaments are woven together by the scarlet thread of the blood covenant to tell one complete story through the Bible.

COME AND DINE

This book takes the mystery and confusion out of the Bible. It provides background information on how we got the Bible, a survey of every book in the Bible and how each relates to Jesus Christ, practical principles, forms and guidelines for your own personal Bible study, and a systematic plan for effectively reading, studying and understanding the Bible for yourself.

WHAT EVERYONE NEEDS TO KNOW ABOUT GOD

This book is about the God of the Bible. It shows the ways in which God has revealed Himself to us and explains the attributes, plans and purposes of God. Then each attribute is related practically to the reader. This book takes you into the very heart of God and demonstrates how to draw near to Him.

RADICAL CHRISTIAN LIVING

This book explains how you can grow to become a mature Christian and help others do so as well. You'll learn the pathway to Christian maturity and how to select and train others in personal follow-up and discipling at different levels of Christian growth.

SEATED IN HEAVENLY PLACES

This book helps the reader learn how to live the victorious Christian life and walk in the power of God. It explains how to minister to others, wear the armor of God and exercise spiritual authority.

BLOW THE TRUMPET IN ZION

This book explains the dramatic story of God's covenant plan for Israel, including their past glory and suffering, their present crisis and their future hope.

JESUS IN THE FEASTS OF ISRAEL

This book is a study of the Old Testament feasts showing how they pointed to Jesus, as well as their personal and prophetic significance for today's world. The book points out how the Feasts represent seven steps to Christian growth and the peace, power and rest of God.

HOW TO PREPARE FOR THE COMING REVIVAL

There is a great expectancy in the hearts of believers everywhere that we are on the threshold of a great revival that will soon shake the world. This book explains the true meaning of revival and what we must do to prepare ourselves for a visitation from God.

SUPERNATURAL PRAYER AND FASTING

In this book Richard uses his clear writing style, God's Word and personal experiences to help us develop a supernatural prayer life.

For a complete catalog of Bible study materials from Richard Booker, visit the website at:

www.rbooker.com

or contact Him at:

Sounds of the Trumpet

4747 Research Forest Drive Ste. 180-330

The Woodlands, TX 77381

Ph: 281-469-1045

Fax: 936-494-1999

BOOK ORDER FORM

To order, copy form and mail to:
Sounds of the Trumpet
4747 Research Forest Dr., #180-330
The Woodlands, TX 77381
Ph: (281) 469-1045   FAX: 936-494-1999
www.rbooker.com   shofarprb@aol.com

☐ Please send me _____ copy(ies) of THE MIRACLE OF THE SCARLET
THREAD. I have enclosed a $12 contribution for each copy ordered (price
includes shipping).

☐ Please send me _____ copy(ies) of COME AND DINE. I have enclosed a
$12 contribution for each copy ordered (price includes shipping).

☐ Please send me _____ copy(ies) of WHAT EVERYONE NEEDS TO
KNOW ABOUT GOD. I have enclosed a $12 contribution for each copy
ordered (price includes shipping).

☐ Please send me _____ copy(ies) of RADICAL CHRISTIAN LIVING. I have
enclosed a $12 contribution for each copy ordered (price includes shipping).

☐ Please send me _____ copy(ies) of SEATED IN HEAVENLY PLACES. I
have enclosed a $12 contribution for each copy ordered (price includes
shipping).

☐ Please send me _____ copy(ies) of BLOW THE TRUMPET IN ZION. I
have enclosed a $12 contribution for each copy ordered (price includes
shipping).

☐ Please send me _____ copy(ies) of JESUS IN THE FEASTS OF ISRAEL.
I have enclosed a $12 contribution for each copy ordered (price includes
shipping).

☐ Please send me _____ copy(ies) of HOW TO PREPARE FOR THE COM-
ING REVIVAL. I have enclosed a $12 contribution for each copy ordered
(price includes shipping).

☐ Foreign orders please include an extra $4.00 per book for surface postage.

_____

Name _____

Street _____

City _____

State _____ Zip _____